Effective Teaching of Religious and Moral Education: Personal Search

Mike Kincaid
Robert McVeigh

Contents

Introduction

HMI inspections over the last five years have revealed that teachers are experiencing difficulties with the Personal Search aspect of 5–14 Religious and Moral Education. Many programmes, say HMI, both at primary and secondary level, do not cover this area satisfactorily, resulting in a lack of pupil attainment. Relevant statements from HMI are included in Appendix 1.

This project is intended to help teachers with this aspect of religious and moral education. It seeks to provide some practical guidance for dealing more effectively with personal search. It is designed to help teachers understand the role of personal search within RME and to provide them with the confidence to develop appropriate learning activities. The project's main purposes are:

- to provide teachers with opportunities to enhance their own professional development in religious and moral education, and especially in relation to personal search
- to provide information, ideas and suggestions for practical teaching.

There are two books and a CD-ROM. One book relates to the National Guidelines, Religious and Moral Education 5–14 and one relates to Religious Education 5–14, Roman Catholic Schools. Each book consists of a series of staff development activities followed by associated reading and teaching exemplars. The CD-ROM contains the text of both books and should enable schools to use the contents for the purposes of staff development.

The staff development activities are aimed at helping teachers become more familiar with personal search as an essential aspect of religious and moral education. They are also aimed at helping teachers improve their practical skills in such areas as questioning, discussion and assessment.

The associated reading consists of information and discussion designed to support the staff development activities. It defines personal search, explains why it is important and suggests a model for teaching it within religious and moral education as a whole. It discusses some of the ways in which teachers can promote personal search in the classroom and provides some practical examples of how it might be assessed. It is concerned with helping teachers to:

- understand the nature and origins of personal search and its place within 5–14 religious and moral education
- appreciate the relationship between personal search and the development of knowledge about religions
- develop understanding of the skills required for personal search and the different types of activity in the classroom that will develop these
- consider assessment of personal search and how judgements about pupil progress and attainment can be made.

The series of twelve exemplars are designed to show how personal search can be introduced in the classroom. They are directed at different levels and stages including level F in order to cover the complete range of 5–14. The exemplars are organised according to three broad stages:

- P1–P3 mainly at Level A
- P4–P6 mainly at levels B/C
- P7–S2 mainly at levels D/E/F.

It is hoped that the staff development activities together with the associated reading and teaching exemplars can have an important, direct and positive impact on pupil achievement and learning.

Part 1: Staff Development Activities

Religious and Moral Education: Personal Search

Part 1: Staff Development Activities

The following series of staff development activities are designed for teachers in primary and secondary schools interested in improving the teaching and learning of religious and moral education in the classroom. The activities can be worked through by individuals or by groups of staff during staff development time. Their intention is to encourage teachers to reflect on their current practice with regard to personal search and to improve their understanding and teaching skills. Opportunities are provided for teachers to discuss the place and significance of personal search within RME, to consider a model for the teaching of personal search and to think about and practise different teaching strategies within the context of their own programme.

The staff development activities are related to and supported by a comprehensive set of notes called 'Associated Reading' that explain and discuss key aspects of religious and moral education with particular reference to personal search. The activities reflect a process of working through the notes in a logical manner and are therefore best completed in the order in which they are set out here. In addition some activities direct teachers to relevant appendices.

Each activity consists of a number of tasks. Some of these will involve personal reading, while others will involve discussion with a colleague or in small groups. There are also practical tasks such as reviewing existing practice, identifying skills and planning a lesson. Teachers should have ready access to the 5–14 RME Guidelines and their own local authority or school programme.

Activity 1: Current practice

Aim: to reflect on current practice in relation to personal search.

Refer to Appendix 1 (p. 67) and read what HMI have to say about the teaching of Personal Search.

Why do you think the Personal Search aspect of Religious and Moral Education has proved to be particularly problematic?

Choose a topic or block of work from your school's 5–14 programme that you have taught recently.

Review the activities you designed for pupils.

What opportunities for personal search can you identify in the tasks you designed?

In what ways could you have improved the personal search aspect of the topic you were teaching?

Activity 2: What is Personal Search?

Aim: to improve understanding of personal search and its place within religious and moral education.

(a)   Read the first section of the Associated Reading headed 'Personal Search' particularly 'Why is it important?' and 'How did it develop?' (pp. 17–18)

Personal search is a process by which pupils can discover and develop their own beliefs and values. *It involves them in* making up their own minds *on religious and moral issues by* developing skills *associated with critical thinking and evaluation.*

Look again at the definition of personal search above. There are three key phrases:
*   discovering and developing beliefs and values
*   making up their own minds
*   developing skills.

In what different ways might young people discover and develop their beliefs and values? What contribution can RME and personal search make to this process?

What are the implications for the effective teaching of personal search if pupils are to develop the ability to 'make up their own minds'?

(b)   Read 'What skills are required?' in the first section of the 'Associated Reading' (pp. 18–19).

In relation to either P1–P3, P4–P6 or P7–S2, make a list of skills which you think are required for personal search?

Within your own school programme identify the opportunities you currently give for pupils to practise these skills.

Discuss your findings with a colleague.

Activity 3: Getting to know the process

Aim: to develop familiarity with the process of personal search.

(a)   Read the second section of the Associated Reading headed 'Personal search and RME – a model' (pp.19–22) that describes the stages of the process. The process has four stages:

- preparing the way
- finding out
- making connections
- thinking it over.

Look at the list of exemplars at the beginning of part 3 'Teaching Exemplars' (pp.33–63). Read through one or more of them from either P1–P3, P4–P6 or P7–S2 paying particular attention to the 'finding out', 'making connections' and 'thinking it over' stages.

Discuss how these three stages interconnect.

(b)   Choose a topic or block of work from your school's 5–14 programme that you have previously taught.

Consider how you went about making connections between the content and pupils' experiences when you last taught it. Were you satisfied with what you did? Why or why not? If not, how might you improve this stage next time round?

Identify a theme which arises from the content and devise a short series of questions you could discuss with pupils as part of the 'thinking it over' stage.

How can you try to ensure that you present the religion being studied 'in the best possible light'? (See the 'Finding out' stage in the second section of the associated reading, headed Personal Search and RME – A Model (p. 21).)

Activity 4: The use of story

Aim: to consider how 'story' can be used to develop personal search.

Read 'Stimulating enquiry' in the third section of the Associated Reading, headed 'Promoting personal search in the classroom' (p. 23).

Read either story A (P1–P3), story B (P4–6) or story C (P7–S2) in Appendix 2 (pp. 68–70).

In small groups discuss how the story could be used to:
* introduce knowledge about a religion
* connect religions and religious information to pupils' own experiences
* think over issues and promote discussion of beliefs and values.

Share the results of your discussion with colleagues.

Activity 5: Asking questions

Aim: to explore the types of questions that can best promote personal search.

(a)   Read 'Asking questions' in the third section of the Associated Reading, 'Promoting personal search in the classroom' (p. 25).

Identify some recent lessons you felt were effective.

Make a list of the typical questions you asked.

How far do they reflect the types of questions set out below?

- Questions that ask for information.
- Questions that focus attention.
- Questions that look for clarification.
- Questions that look for reasons.
- Questions that relate the content to pupils' own experiences.
- Questions that explore the issues.

In addition you might wish to invite a colleague to observe a lesson and to comment on your use of questions.

To what extent were the questions you asked 'open' or 'closed'? What was the purpose of the 'open' questions?

(b)   In twos or threes plan a lesson in which most of the questions are 'open' questions designed to encourage pupils' thinking and personal search.

Share what you have produced with the rest of the staff or department.

Activity 6: Engaging pupils in discussion

Aim: to examine alternative strategies for engaging pupils in discussion.

(a)   Read 'Creating a thinking environment' and 'Providing positive feedback' in the third section of the Associated Reading, 'Promoting personal search in the classroom' (pp. 23–25).

What factors do you think might inhibit pupils from expressing their views freely?

What could you do to encourage them?

Read 'Engaging pupils in discussion' that is also part of the section 'Promoting personal search in the classroom' (pp. 25–26). Pay particular attention to the different strategies outlined there.

- Buzz sessions
- Brainstorming
- Round table discussion groups
- Rainbow groups
- Twos to fours
- Listening triads

Which of the strategies, if any, have you previously used? How successful did you find them?

What other strategies can you think of that might help pupils to engage in discussion more effectively?

Identify a block of work or a topic you are about to teach.

Describe to a partner how you might introduce at least one of the strategies.

Teach the block of work and evaluate the success of the strategy against the following criteria:
- pupils listened and responded to what others had to say
- pupils tried to build on the suggestions of others where appropriate
- their comments on the whole were relevant and to the point
- they showed a willingness when appropriate to challenge the views of others and allowed their own views to be open to scrutiny
- they were able to put across what they wanted to say without being domineering and to be critical without being aggressive.

Activity 7: Assessing personal search

Aims: to explore current assessment practice.
To consider different ways in which to assess personal search.

(a)   Read 'Purposes of assessment' in the fourth section of the Associated Reading headed 'Assessing personal search' (p. 27).

Which of the following does your current practice usually involve assessing?

- Knowledge
- Understanding
- Skills
- Attitudes

What forms of evidence does your assessment usually involve?

- Observation
- Discussion
- Written work
- Test

Discuss the reasons for your answers with a partner.

(b)   Read 'Forms of assessment' in the fourth section of the Associated Reading (pp. 28–29).

Refer to the Personal Search targets in the 5–14 RME Guidelines or in your own local authority or school programme.

In relation to one or two of these indicate what you might want to talk to pupils about in order to help them with their learning.

What might you be looking for in terms of a response?

(c)   Choose a block of work you have taught recently and prepare the outline of a task you could set pupils to find out how well they have done. The task could cover knowledge and understanding as well as personal search.

Or

Identify one or two personal search targets from the 5–14 Guidelines or your own programme and consider what kind of evidence you would look for when assessing them and why.

Part 2: Associated Reading

Part 2: Associated Reading

1. Personal search

The importance of personal search in religious and moral education is clearly evident in the aims section of the 5–14 RME Guidelines. The guidelines set out four aims for religious and moral education one of which deals with personal search. They link personal search with the idea that pupils should be helped to form their own beliefs and values by developing certain skills. The aims are to help pupils to:

- develop a knowledge and understanding of Christianity and other world religions and to recognise religion as an important expression of human experience
- appreciate moral values such as honesty, liberty, justice, fairness and concern for others
- investigate and understand the questions and answers that religions can offer about the nature and meaning of life
- develop their own beliefs, attitudes, moral values and practices through a process of personal search, discovery and critical evaluation.

Definition
Personal search is a process by which pupils can discover and develop their own beliefs and values. It involves them in making up their own minds on religious and moral issues by developing skills associated with critical thinking and evaluation.

Why is it important?
Up until the 1960s the aims of religious education were explicitly Christian. It was generally assumed that all children were Christian and came from Christian homes. Consequently it seemed sufficient for religious education to familiarise pupils with the content and beliefs of the Bible. In a survey of schools conducted by the Millar Committee towards the end of the sixties, the main content of religious education programmes was found to be Bible stories and Bible knowledge. When asked whether they used any textbook other than the Bible, almost 80 per cent of schools replied, 'No, or very rarely'.

Gradually, however, it became apparent that traditional Christianity was losing much of its hold on the thoughts and emotions of a great many people. Many believed that there was a widening gap between the beliefs of traditional Christianity and the beliefs and opinions of ordinary people. Religion was coming to be regarded by society not as a fixed set of doctrines to be accepted by everyone and transmitted to the next generation but as an open search for truth and a matter of personal choice. Pupils could not be told the answers to religious questions because there was no agreement among adults as to what the answers were. Since religious belief was an open-ended matter, religious education in schools also had to be open-ended. It could no longer be aimed at producing assent to a particular set of beliefs or commitment to one particular faith. It had to involve a personal search and pupils had to be encouraged to make up their own minds on religious questions and issues.

Unlike previous generations young people today have no ready-made framework of beliefs and values that they can easily identify and assimilate as their own. There is no set of agreed beliefs and values that everyone adheres to and accepts. The breakdown of consensus is particularly evident from the 1960s but today young people face an even greater proliferation of personal, social and ideological choices. The rapid growth of world-wide telecommunications, for example, means that people from almost anywhere in the world can talk to each other and exchange ideas about beliefs and lifestyles. The decline of Christianity as the main source of moral and religious authority has meant that people, both young and old, no longer automatically look to the churches for help in making sense of and responding to the uncertainty and unpredictability of life. A curriculum that is designed to assist pupils with their own search and help them to make up their own minds about beliefs and values is more important than ever.

How did it develop?

In Scotland the view that personal search should be a major element in religious education was significantly developed by the Curriculum Guidelines of 1981. Commonly referred to as Bulletin 2, it stated that in religious education the major insights of religions should always be related to the pupils' own search. In order to help teachers translate this principle into practical activities for pupils, the authors of Bulletin 2 recommended two sets of objectives:

• those relating to religions and other stances for living

• those relating to the questions and issues that arise within pupils' own experience and within human experience generally.

The latter included questions of morality arising particularly from personal and social relationships and issues relating to rights and responsibilities. It also included questions of meaning and purpose arising from human existence and from the natural world – where does life from come from originally? Does my life have a purpose? What happens after death? How did the universe come into being? Is there a God?

In its rationale for religious education the National Guidelines for 5–14 RME highlight two factors. First of all religion is a significant area of human experience and as such it deserves to be studied by pupils. In particular, they argue, the Christian religion has had an important impact on the history and traditions of Scotland and continues to exert an influence on national life. Although Christianity is recognised as the major religious tradition of this country, pupils are also to be encouraged to develop understanding of other faiths. Consequently, programmes of study should also include the study of religions such as Buddhism, Hinduism, Islam, Judaism and Sikhism.

Second, there is a personal dimension to the study of religions that is linked to the individual's ability to find his or her own answers to religious questions and issues. The questions and answers that emerge within their own experience, including the home and community, have to be related to the various expressions of belief and practice found in the great religions of the world. In this way, say the guidelines, the two sides of religious education, the 'objective or study of religions side' and the 'subjective or personal search side', can be brought together.

What skills are required?

The definition of personal search states that making up one's mind on religious and moral issues involves the development of skills associated with critical thinking and evaluation. Critical thinking and evaluation are central to the teaching and assessment of certificate courses available from S3 onwards. The 5–14 RME guidelines suggest that teachers should keep in mind an overview of what is expected for 14–18 particularly when thinking about programmes for pupils beyond Level E.

In 5–14 RME most of the skills to be developed are arranged under the strands relating to *natural world*, *relationships and moral values*, and *ultimate questions*, although some are also to be found among the strands of *Christianity* and *Other World Religions*. These skills can be thought of as contributing to and supporting the development of critical thinking and evaluation. One of the key skills of evaluation that students studying Standard Grade and Intermediate

Level courses are expected to demonstrate is the ability 'to identify and discuss arguments on both sides of an issue'. Some of the skills that might contribute to and support the development of this ability appear as personal search targets at most levels. For example:

- listening to the views of others and expressing their own views
- giving reasons for the opinions they put forward
- showing awareness of alternative viewpoints
- applying principles and values to real and imaginary situations.

Other skills among the personal search targets are introduced using words such as 'respond' and 'reflect'. At Level B pupils are expected to respond to situations involving values such as fairness and honesty. Respond here might mean:

- saying how they felt about a situation in their own experience
- talking about what might happen in a situation and whether it would be good or bad.

At Level A and Level B pupils are expected to be able to share their ideas and feelings and 'respond to different aspects of the natural world'. Respond here might mean:

- giving an example
- giving a reason
- stating a preference.

Reflect as in 'reflect, with support, on the natural order of the human life-cycle: birth, growth, maturity, death in association with religious ceremonies marking these stages' (Level C) and 'reflect, with support, on the significance of life on planet earth in relation to the vastness of the universe' (Level D). This might involve pupils in:

- expressing a relevant point clearly
- asking a relevant question
- making a comparison
- explaining an argument in their own words.

2. Personal search and RME – a model

Religious and Moral Education then includes both the study of religions and personal search. According to Bulletin 2 and the 5–14 National Guidelines these different aspects of religious and moral education need to be brought together if a coherent curriculum is to be created. While acknowledging the significant part played by Bulletin 2 and the 5–14 National Guidelines in developing personal search, it is the intention of this project to move beyond both in at least one important respect. The project introduces a model that draws together the two aspects of religious education – the study of religions and personal search. The model is designed to help pupils understand and appreciate religions and at the same time contribute to the development of their own beliefs and values. The process consists essentially of creating a dialogue within the classroom between the pupils' own beliefs, values and assumptions and the systems of beliefs, values and practices represented by the world's major religions.

The world's major religious traditions provide an indispensable source of information and dialogue for individuals interested in developing their own beliefs and values. Anyone seriously interested in discovering and developing beliefs and values must confront at some point the world's great religions and in particular their scriptures. The process of formulating beliefs and values requires a growing knowledge of religious, moral and philosophical viewpoints for without such input our own beliefs and values will remain unchallenged, undeveloped and uninformed.

The process

The process is designed to enable pupils to go beyond just finding out what other people believe. It involves pupils first of all entering into the thoughts and feelings of believers by allowing the symbols, artefacts, festivals and stories of their religions to work on their imaginations. They are encouraged to find out and gather in new things to think about – beliefs, values, viewpoints, perspectives. Through discussion and other activities they are helped to connect these with their own ideas and experiences and to consider some of the questions and issues that may be of concern to them. In this way they can begin to form, strengthen and develop their own beliefs, values and ways of behaving.

The process has four stages.

*   Preparing the way
*   Finding out
*   Making connections
*   Thinking it over

The four stages of the process may not always take place in the order that they are set out above, although the first stage of 'preparing the way' will usually precede the other three. In some instances it may be important to make connections with an aspect of pupil experience at the beginning of a block of work before going on to introduce material from the religion being studied. It may also be that discussion and activities frequently move backwards and forwards between 'finding out' and 'making connections'. Questions and discussion about pupils' own experiences or about the issues arising from the religious and moral content may occur at any time at the teacher's initiative or in response to points made by pupils themselves.

Blocks of work incorporating the process might be included in the wider study of a specific religion or be part of a topic that focuses on an aspect of human experience but that makes important links with the religions of the world. They might also be part of topics that focus on aspects of different religions such as signs and symbols, holy books, religious leaders, pilgrimages, which are taken to be common to all religions. They might also be taught alongside topics in other areas of the curriculum particularly environmental studies. Creation and caring for the environment for example might be part of a wider theme on aspects of the environment while the study of a place of worship could be part of a wider study of the local area.

Preparing the way

The first stage involves preparing for learning through a sharing of information and objectives. Pupils need to see how new work is linked to work they have already done. Some opportunity for them to bring to mind what they already know will make them more receptive to new and related information.

They need to be given an overview of the content and the order in which it is to be tackled. This could include reference to the main issues that will arise and that will be the basis of activities for thinking and evaluating. It should also include a list of key words and terms that pupils are likely to come across in their study.

The learning outcomes should be shared and talked about so that pupils are clear what they are expected to have achieved by the end of a particular block of learning. They also need to know what is expected of them as far as class assignments, homework and assessment is concerned.

This stage is also about ensuring that there is a stimulating environment to support the learning activities. This might mean making sure that the resources to be used during the theme are available for pupils to see – videos, textbooks, artefacts, photographs and posters, indeed anything connected with the learning that might stimulate interest and motivation.

Finding out

This stage involves finding out about the beliefs, values and practices of religious traditions. It is virtually impossible to develop the abilities to express ideas and engage in critical thinking without first establishing a firm basis in relevant knowledge and understanding. Pupils need to be encouraged therefore not only to acquire and retain knowledge but to appreciate the importance of knowledge and evidence as the basis for expressing and justifying their opinions.

Within the study of religion, Christianity, in its various forms, will always have an important place in the curriculum. It is the religion that pupils are most likely to meet in the community and it has been a significant force in shaping our values and way of life. Other religions too will have an important role to play in helping pupils to develop their own beliefs and values and to develop understanding of and respect for people of all faiths. The tradition of enquiry into religion, on which religious and moral education is dependent, has served to clarify considerably the nature and structure of religions. One such framework is used in the 5–14 RME guidelines where religions are said to consist of five strands:

*   Celebrations, festivals, ceremonies and customs
*   Sacred writings, stories and key figures
*   Beliefs
*   Sacred places, worship and symbols
*   Moral values and attitudes.

This framework can help us to identify the distinctive beliefs, values and practices that each religion offers its adherents. Pupils can find out something of what it means to be a Christian, a Hindu, a Jew, discover what religions believe about the world and encounter different views about how human life should be lived. There is also an experiential aspect to religions that is equally important. For religious believers awareness of the 'sacred' can be brought about by participation in community worship, individual prayer and meditation, as well as through the religious interpretation of their own human experiences.

Pupils of all ages will come to the study of religion with their own perspectives, their own framework of beliefs, values and ways of behaving. We can never approach religions in a neutral or completely objective fashion. This does not mean, however, that we cannot succeed in understanding the religious or cultural worlds of others. Nor does it mean that as teachers we are conditioned to distort other faiths and cultural traditions. Naturally, we may on occasions misunderstand the meaning of a festival or the significance of a belief, and consequently misrepresent it to those whom we are teaching. What is important is that we have as a central principle the intention to present religions in the 'best possible light'. Understanding is rarely an all or nothing thing. Thus the 5–14 RME guidelines state that some pupils, by the time they complete their second year of secondary education, should be able to show *some* understanding of Christian beliefs such as incarnation, salvation and life after death (Level E).

Making connections

This stage involves relating the knowledge and insights gained to pupils' own ideas and life experiences. In the rationale of the *Structure and Balance of the Curriculum: 5–14 National Guidelines* it states that a curriculum should build on pupils' experience and learning and relate to events and facets of their everyday lives. This fits well with the importance religious and moral education has always placed on relating religious beliefs, values and practices to pupils' own experiences and everyday life.

Pupils' experiences of family, friendships and being part of a local community have already begun to shape their intellectual, social and moral development. They have already learned much about themselves and their world and have taken on a range of beliefs, values and ways of behaving. Religious and moral education can build on this by introducing pupils to a wider range of belief systems and by providing opportunities for them, within a supportive environment, to reflect on and talk about their own related ideas and experiences. In this way pupils can gain some insight into the beliefs and values of religious believers and begin to identify the wider questions and issues that may be of concern to them.

It is important that pupils are provided with 'real' time to review what they have learned, if they are to relate it to their own ideas and experiences. Research into the way the brain learns suggests that providing personal processing time after new learning is critical if that learning is to be effective. Continually moving pupils on from one piece of learning to another virtually guarantees that little will be learned or retained. Pupils could be involved in class or small group discussion to sort out in their own minds what they have been learning, to generate questions and clarify points. Alternatively, in response to questions posed by the teacher, they could be asked to write up their own notes or include in a journal some personal comments on the relevance of the material to their own lives.

Thinking it over

Thinking it over is the climax of the process. This stage involves thinking about and evaluating some of the questions and issues arising from their study of religion and their own experiences. Pupils are encouraged to discuss the issues raised and, by gradually developing a range of skills, they can further their personal search and begin to develop their own framework of beliefs and values.

Thinking it over should be challenging, dealing with issues that push children's thinking beyond the immediate knowledge of the content. The issues should invite discussion on a range of questions to do with God, suffering, life and death, relationships, moral and social values, and the nature and origins of the natural world. They will arise in the main from a consideration of the beliefs, values, practices, stories and key figures associated with the religious traditions being studied.

Learning to think about and evaluate issues involves the development of a number of key attitudes and dispositions. For example, it involves a willingness to engage in discussion with others whose points of view may be different from one's own. It involves having the confidence to challenge the ideas of others and in turn be willing to submit one's own views to scrutiny and the challenge of reason. It also means being prepared to review what one previously thought and valued. Pupils who are not willing or able to listen to what others have to say or to give reasons for their own ideas when asked by others are unlikely to be able to reflect on their own views sufficiently to develop their own beliefs and values.

3. Promoting personal search in the classroom

Teachers can promote pupils' personal search by:
• stimulating enquiry
• creating a thinking environment
• providing positive feedback
• asking questions
• engaging pupils in discussion.

The process set out in the previous section is designed to enable pupils to appreciate religions and other stances for living, and to develop their beliefs and values. Discovering and developing one's own beliefs and values, personal search, is an integral part of religious and moral education. It involves individuals in relating their growing knowledge of religions to their own interests and concerns and in thinking through the religious and moral issues that arise, both from within the content itself and from their own experience of life. An essential part of the process therefore is the finding and understanding of relevant information.

Stimulating enquiry

Teachers can stimulate enquiry through the provision of first-hand experience – visits to places of worship, being visited by a representative of a local religion within the community or through artefacts brought into the classroom. It will also include providing appropriate materials within the classroom. This can involve material from a published scheme, books, radio and television programmes, computer programmes and material provided personally by the teacher. It might involve a short discussion about some of the artefacts relating to Christian communion – the communion table or altar, the communion cup or chalice, the bread and wine, the words of Jesus as described in the New Testament. Or it might begin with some discussion based on a picture of a Hindu god such as Ganesh. Ganesh is usually depicted with an elephant's head and has a rat as a constant companion. He is particularly worshipped as the god who can help to overcome problems and protect people from harm.

Another way of stimulating enquiry is through the use of stories. It is characteristic of religions to have stories. They are an important part of how religions express their identity. Stories pull together experiences and memories of the past and recreate them for believers. Stories often serve as the background to religious ceremonies and festivals: the Exodus from Egypt, the Last Supper, the story of Rama and Sita. One of the most important functions of stories within religions is to explain the origins of the universe and humankind. Their purpose is usually to define, in religious and philosophical terms, the place and significance of human beings in the world, and in this way provide people with answers to questions about meaning and purpose in life. Pupils can apply stories to their own lives and interpret them according to their own experiences. Stories can provide them with different ideas, beliefs and opinions to discuss and argue about. Through stories pupils can enter into, and learn from, the experiences of others.

Pupils should also be encouraged to find information for themselves. The effective use of dictionaries, indices and contents pages will be important if they are to easily find the information they want. They also need to develop the skills of accessing information from content-based packages such as CD-ROMs and also, through the internet, the world wide web. They require opportunities to practise and apply these skills in a variety of contexts. This means that they need to be engaged in research as part of their usual means of learning.

Creating a thinking environment

Pupils' sense of identity and belonging is intimately related to what they believe and to the values that affect their thoughts and actions. It follows that, if pupils are to think for themselves and express their own views, it is vital that in the process their sense of identity and belonging are not adversely affected. From the point of view of pupils the practice of encouraging them to think for themselves and express their own views can bring with it a considerable degree of risk. In particular it may be the risk of making a mistake, of being seen as different, of being in a minority of one.

If we want to build the right atmosphere here we need first to encourage pupils to take risks. This will mean making clear to pupils that making mistakes is inevitable, particularly when exploring new ideas and discussing difficult issues. It will also mean encouraging them to challenge the teacher's ideas and ways of thinking as well as the views they encounter in books and other resources. This will help the process of moving to a situation where the pupils become willing to submit their own ideas to the challenge of others. Pupils also need to feel that their comments and opinions will be respected, that originality and difference are things to be valued and that their views and interests count.

Teachers need to help pupils to develop an attitude of open-mindedness so that they can learn to live with some degree of ambiguity. Being open-minded, however, does not mean having no beliefs or convictions or for that matter having to be permanently indecisive. It means being prepared to listen to other points of view, to consider new evidence, and to be willing to change or amend one's opinion if there seem to be sufficient reason. From early primary pupils need to be discouraged from regarding every question they come across as having only one single correct answer. Instead they need to be encouraged to go on thinking, to hypothesise and suggest new possibilities.

Creating a thinking environment also involves encouraging pupils to talk, to take part in discussion, to exchange views and respond to a range of opinions. It is particularly important when thinking about and evaluating religious and moral issues that pupils are exposed to points of view that are different from their own. Among the important skills that pupils need to develop here are the abilities to listen carefully to what others are saying, to keep to the point, and build on other people's suggestions.

If pupils are to develop their ability to think about religious and moral issues it is also important that they see the relevance of what they are learning. By discussing and writing about religious and moral questions pupils can be involved in thinking about the beliefs and values that are important to them. For the teacher this means taking account of what children already know, their curiosities, their problems, interests and experiences, and showing how these relate to what is being studied, and how such study can provide answers that will help them lead more satisfying lives.

To create a thinking environment teachers should:
* make the learning relevant to pupils' own interests and experiences
* highlight the issues in order to challenge them and make them think
* help pupils to feel that their comments are respected and that their views and opinions count
* encourage them to challenge the views of others and to allow their own views to be open to scrutiny
* encourage pupils to put across their own point of view without being domineering and to be critical without becoming aggressive.

Providing positive feedback
One important way of contributing to pupils' abilities to think about religious and moral issues is for teachers and everyone in the class to provide positive feedback. Research has shown that children are influenced by comments from other people, particularly those whom they consider to be important to them. Younger children in particular are greatly influenced by the evaluations of themselves by adults. Older children regard the evaluations they got from their peer group and friends as much more important.

The nature of the feedback that they get from these 'important' people affects their self-esteem and their ability to achieve. If teachers show that they expect pupils to work hard, take part in discussion and generally do well, there is more likelihood that this will happen. Teachers therefore need to engage directly with individuals, groups and the whole class as much as possible, helping pupils to deepen their understandings and encouraging them to express and justify their opinions on the issues and questions that arise from their enquiries. It also important to draw attention to what is good and give appropriate praise and encouragement.

Responding to pupils' ideas and views in different ways is important if we are to help them to develop their abilities to think about religious and moral issues. For example, if a situation is concerned with facts that are incorrect or information that is misleading, then this needs to be clearly pointed out to pupils. If, on the other hand, a situation concerns pupils' interpretations, understandings, judgements and opinions, then a more appropriate response will be one that is much less definite with the intention of encouraging pupils to go on thinking. When providing feedback teachers need to be careful not to 'close off' pupils' thinking by always trying to sum up or to offer their own solutions. Because they have the authority of the teacher these suggestions may be regarded as the 'right' answers and may inhibit further thinking. Even at the end of a general discussion or debate teachers should avoid the temptation of always providing their own evaluation on the virtue of the ideas that have been put forward. It is often better to leave things open to some extent so that pupils go away still thinking, than to give the class the impression that the last word has been spoken and nothing further remains to be said on the subject.

Providing positive feedback for personal search involves:

- engaging pupils as much as possible in discussion individually, within groups and with the whole class
- listening and responding to pupils' answers in ways that encourage them to go on thinking
- drawing attention to what is good and giving appropriate praise and encouragement.

Asking questions

Questioning is an important part of the teacher's role, particularly when helping pupils to relate the content and stories of religions to their own experience and when encouraging them to think about the issues. Questioning can initiate and maintain discussion, encouraging pupils to talk about their own ideas, attitudes and experiences. Although on occasions teachers' question will be of the 'closed' variety inviting recall of what pupils have learned, most of the questioning will be 'open' with the intention of stimulating their thinking.

Careful thought should be given to the sequence of questions so that pupils can, as far as possible, build on information and ideas that they have already discussed. Rephrasing questions, providing helpful clues and examples, and acknowledging relevant answers are also ways in which teachers can promote good discussion. Suitable pacing of questions that allows pupils to process their responses is also important. If we want pupils to think for themselves we need to give them time to consider things. During periods of discussion there is always a great temptation to wait only a few seconds after having asked a question before asking someone else or even providing the answer. Short waiting times are likely to encourage short answers, whereas allowing more time is more likely to produce responses of greater length.

The main types of questions in religious and moral education are:

- questions that ask for information – for example in the story of the Buddha teachers might want to remind pupils of aspects of the content; with what three aspects of life did the Buddha come face to face?
- questions that focus attention – this might be in relation to a television/radio programme, a picture or a story; what do you notice? What else do you see? What are they doing? What do you find particularly interesting about? Why do you think that? Such questions open up areas for investigation and help pupils to focus on particular details.
- questions that look for clarification – What do you mean by? Can you explain that a bit more? Can you give me an example? Can you put that another way? These questions stimulate and extend pupils thinking by helping them to clarify what they mean and express points more fully.
- questions that look for reasons – Why do you think that? What evidence is there? What other views are there? How is your way of looking at things different from?
- questions that relate the content to pupils' own experiences – Why do you think Siddharta felt he had to leave his family and give up all his wealth? Would you be prepared to give up anything in order to help others?
- questions that explore the issues – Do we have a duty to help people in need? Is helping others our responsibility or the government's?

Engaging pupils in discussion

Discussion is essential for religious and moral education and particularly for personal search. By engaging in dialogue with individuals, groups and the whole class, the teacher can help pupils to develop their abilities to think about and evaluate religious and moral issues. The opportunity for pupils to talk within a formal setting with others who may have different beliefs and experiences from their own will help to widen their view of the issues under discussion, as well as help them to see things from a different perspective.

Fruitful discussion can take place at any stage of the process. It might be at the 'finding out' stage for example, when pupils are discovering together some information, encountering artefacts or interacting with some video or computer programme. Discussion will also be important when helping pupils to relate aspects of religions to their own experience and when talking over the issues that have arisen from what is being studied.

The HMI report on effective learning and teaching in religious education (1994) found that whole-class discussion was effective when it was conducted at a suitable pace and was supported with good open-ended questioning. This had the effect of stimulating and challenging pupils, encouraging them to become more thoughtfully involved in the lesson. Although whole class discussions can be useful for engaging the attention of all pupils, it does not allow sufficient space for pupils to explore issues in depth. Group talk particularly in relation to open-ended issues therefore will always be important. Wherever there is a range of viewpoints to be found, different possibilities to be explored, depths of meaning to be uncovered, the opportunity to talk through these in small groups will be important. Provided the right climate exists, engaging in this kind of group discussion will give pupils the opportunity to express their ideas and test them out.

Important for effective group discussion is the opportunity for groups to present their ideas and conclusions to the whole class. This can have a significant effect on the group. Members become conscious of having to be much clearer in the way they organise their thoughts and conclusions since these have to be presented to others who have not been party to the discussions. This 'reporting back' will serve to iron out some of the tentativeness of much early discussion forcing them to clarify some things while elaborating on others. Preparation too is vital particularly in the form of a stimulus for the discussion. This can provide a helpful 'point of return' if discussion falters or proceeds up a blind alley towards a dead end.

One of the challenges involved in organising group discussion is ensuring that individuals feel satisfied with their own contribution. Some will begin the discussion well but find that they cannot sustain it for any length of time. As a result the outcome of the discussion process is minimal and pupils can often come to regard the exercise as frustrating and a waste of time. It is here that the use of 'content prompts' can be useful. These prompts or triggers provide brief statements expressing commonly held viewpoints on an issue. Each member of a group can be given two or three content prompts that they can then use to enhance their contributions to the group discussion. The content prompts can be used verbatim or pupils can adapt them and use their own words. They can also have the effect of sparking off their own ideas.

The following strategies can be useful for developing personal search.

- *Buzz sessions* – for building confidence and encouraging risk taking, buzz sessions are particularly valuable. Here the intention is to create a climate in which students can feel able to express their opinions without fear of being 'wrong' or being ridiculed in any way. There will usually be no formal report back or taking of notes.
- *Brainstorming* – brainstorming can also be a useful technique. Students work in groups where the idea is for each member to think up as many ideas as possible about an issue. Individual contributions are gathered together without any attempt initially to categorise them or establish a priority. Once the brainstorm is complete, groups should turn to the task of thinking more critically about the ideas that have emerged, so that some basis for choosing what is relevant or important is established.
- *Round table discussion groups* – here four or five pupils will sit around a table and discuss an issue. At the end there will be a formal report back to the whole class.
- *Rainbow groups* – each pupil in a group is given a number or a colour. When the group has worked together, all the pupils with the same number or colour form new groups to compare what they have done.
- *Twos to fours* – pupils work initially in pairs before joining with another pair to compare notes. This provides a valuable opportunity to explain their own points of view and respond to the views of the others.
- *Listening triads* – pupils take on the roles of talker, questioner or recorder. The talker explains their own point of view on an issue or comments more generally on both sides of an issue. The questioner seeks clarification and asks questions. The recorder takes notes and at the end of the time gives a report of the conversation. Next time the roles are changed.

4. Assessing personal search

Purposes of assessment

Assessment is an important part of the teaching and learning process. If a block of work is planned in relation to certain targets it is necessary to assess how far these targets have been achieved. Assessment can take place in any context where pupils are completing or have completed tasks in relation to stated targets. It can be done formally by means of a written test or a specially devised piece of written work that is marked – or informally during regular classroom work where the teacher listens to a group of pupils discussing an issue or talks individually to a pupil.

The assessment of personal search is not at all concerned with making judgements about pupils' personal beliefs and values. It is simply not appropriate to assess whether pupils' own beliefs are right or wrong. If teachers are to help pupils with their learning in relation to personal search and make judgements about the overall quality of their work, they need to focus on the development of skills. Thus pupils' views on a religious or moral issue should not be assessed as right or wrong, although the skills involved in arriving at that view (giving reasons for their opinions, showing awareness of alternative views) may be assessed. The main purposes of assessment are:

- to help pupils to learn
- to gather evidence of their progress.

Helping pupils to learn should focus on the continuing assessment of pupils' learning in the classroom at regular intervals. It deals with the immediate content pupils are working on and is intended to help them develop their understanding and think more clearly about the issues. It involves the teacher directly in providing positive feedback to pupils, informing them about what they have done well and offering advice concerning the next steps in their learning. Although it may be informal it should nevertheless be part of a planned and systematic approach. This might involve taking time out to pay 'special attention' to a particular group of pupils on a regular basis. Teachers should:

- be clear which target or targets are being assessed
- ensure that the rest of the class is purposefully engaged
- decide which pupils to talk to and for how long
- acknowledge success by giving appropriate praise and encouragement
- use the results as the basis for deciding next steps in learning
- record the results and use them as part of an ongoing running record of progress.

A second main purpose of assessment is to gather evidence about pupils' progress. It refers to the information teachers get from assessments. It is important to retain some of that information so that when teachers draw conclusions for parents and others they can do so on the basis of what pupils actually achieved. There are two main ways of obtaining evidence about achievements:

- summing up
- checking up.

Summing up pulls together the information recorded over a period of time from the informal but systematic assessments conducted by the teacher. It is likely that these assessments will be the same ones used to help pupils with their learning. The summing up will be based on the brief notes and comments from observation of and discussion with pupils, together with some evidence of their class work. These are now taken together to provide a picture of pupils' achievements at a point in time.

Checking up is usually carried out by setting a test or specially devised task at the end of a topic to find out what pupils have learned. Tests that sample the content covered in a topic allow all pupils to demonstrate what they have learned but tend to emphasise the recall of knowledge, albeit with some understanding. Specially devised tasks can provide opportunities for pupils to show how they can apply their knowledge in new and unfamiliar contexts.

Forms of assessment

Assessment of personal search is likely to take three main forms.

- Listening to group discussion
- Talking with individual pupils
- Specially devised tasks

Listening to group discussion

Some targets can be assessed while the teacher is listening to a group discussing an issue. Among the targets that might be assessed this way are 'listen to the views of others and express their own with growing articulateness' (Levels C and D, Ultimate Questions); 'express and discuss questions about the origins of the world' (Level D, Natural World); 'discuss issues relating to creation, miracles, resurrection at a simple level' (Level E, Sacred Writings, Stories and Key Figures).

Let us suppose that a class of P7 pupils have been looking at the story of how Jesus was arrested in the garden of Gethsemane. They have been finding out about some of the events that led to his arrest and the reasons he had become unpopular with some sections of society. They have considered ideas like commitment, sacrifice and some of the teaching of Jesus relating to loving one's enemies. The pupils have a sheet summarising this information and providing some starter questions and prompts. They form round table discussion groups to discuss the issue of whether Jesus' disciples were right to defend him by force. From her observations the teacher notes how well pupils:

- listen to what is being said
- respond appropriately (without being aggressive or domineering)
- express their own opinions (and give reasons).

Talking with individual pupils

Most targets are amenable to a form of assessment where the teacher talks to pupils individually. For example, pupils are asked to offer a personal response, reflect with support, express their own questions and opinions or respond to beliefs or values contained in stories and real or imaginary situations. In the following examples the teacher might introduce the conversation by briefly reviewing work already done and pointing to previous successes. In addition, as appropriate, the teacher can prompt pupils along the way, ask subsidiary questions and remind them of relevant information they may have forgotten.

1. In relation to the target 'offer a personal response to the variety, order and beauty of the world' (Level A, Natural World): The teacher asks pupils to draw a picture of their favourite season and say what they particularly like about it.

2. In relation to 'respond to ideas of fairness, honesty, respect for others in stories and real incidents' (Level B, Relationships and Moral Values): The teacher asks pupils to tell them about a time when they thought they were being treated unfairly and how it made them feel.

3. In relation to 'recognise situations involving moral conflict, show awareness of alternative viewpoints and be able to offer a personal opinion, backed by reasons' (Level E, Relationships and Moral Values): The teacher asks pupils to:
   - explain what the moral issue is in relation to vegetarianism
   - state briefly one point of view other than their own
   - express their own opinion and give a reason.

Specially devised tasks

As we have already mentioned specially devised tasks are most appropriate for checking up on what pupils have learned at the end of a block of work or topic. They also allow scope for pupils to show how they can apply what they have learned in a different context. Two examples of personal search targets together with associated tasks are set out below. These are also linked to related targets of knowledge and understanding in 'Other World Religions'.

Reflect with support on the natural order of the human life cycle – birth, growth, maturity, death – in association with religious ceremonies marking these stage. (Level C, Natural World)

You are a reporter for a local weekly newspaper and your editor has obtained permission for you to attend a Bar/Bat Mitzvah ceremony. He has told you to prepare a report for the next issue. You are to include:
- a description of the ceremony
- the meaning attached to the special items used and worn at the ceremony
- an explanation of the importance of the ceremony for the boy/girl and for the Jewish community
- your views on whether or not 12/13-year-olds can be considered responsible young adults.

Be able to express and discuss questions about the origins of the world and relate them to religious stories of creation (Level D, Natural World).

Pupils are presented with a religious story of creation that they have not seen before. They are asked to read the story and answer the following questions:
- Which of the following elements are represented in the story? – a designer, the origin of human life, the causes of suffering, evil.
- In what ways is the importance of human beings shown in the story?
- Why do you think people all over the world made up stories about how everything began?
- Does it matter how the universe began? Why or why not?

References and bibliography

Costello, P., *Thinking Skills and Early Childhood Education*, David Fulton, 2000

Cox, E., *Changing Aims in Religious Education*, Routledge, 1966

Dean, J., *Organising Learning in the Primary School*, Routledge,1983

Fisher, R., Teaching *Children to Think*, Blackwell, 1990

Galton, M. and Williamson, J., *Group Work in the Primary Classroom*, Routledge, 1992

HM Inspectors of Schools, *Effective Learning and Teaching in Scottish Primary and Secondary Schools: Religious Education*, SOED, 1994

Hopkins, D. and Harris, A., *Creating the Conditions for Teaching and Learning*, David Fulton, 2000

Markham, I., *A World Religions Reader*, Blackwell, 1996

Moon, B. and Shelton Mayes, A. (eds) *Teaching and Learning in the Secondary School*, Open University, 1994, chapters 33 and 34

Scottish Central Committee on Religious Education Curriculum *Guidelines for Religious Education*, Bulletin 2, Consultative Committee on the Curriculum, 1981

Scottish Education Department, *Moral and Religious Education in Scottish Schools*, Millar Report, SED, 1972

Scottish Executive *The Structure and Balance of the Curriculum: 5–14* National Guidelines, Learning and Teaching Scotland, 2000

Scottish Office Education Department, *Religious and Moral Education: 5–14 National Guidelines*, SOED, 1992

Wright, A. and Brandon, A. M. (eds) *Learning to Teach Religious Education in the Secondary School*, Routledge, 2000, especially chapters 3, 4 and 6

Part 3: Teaching Exemplars

Part 3: Teaching Exemplars

The exemplars are designed in accordance with three broad stages across 5–14, P1–P3 mainly at Level A, P4–P6 mainly at levels B/C and P7–S2 mainly at levels D/E/F.

For P1–P3 the exemplars relate to:
- Birth of the Buddha
- Christmas
- Guru Nanak
- Raksha Bandhan.

For P4–P6 the exemplars focus on:
- Ceremonies in Hinduism – beginning the journey of life
- The Sangha
- A visit to a Church of Scotland parish church
- Zakah and Muslim aid.

For P7–S2 the exemplars are:
- The Sikh Langar
- Yom Kippur and the story of Jonah
- Exploring Christian beliefs about creation
- Muhammad, the Prophet of Islam.

Each exemplar is set out in a similar way spread over a double page. The left-hand page contains the title, the broad stage to which it relates and several targets from the 5–14 RME National Guidelines. The targets will include relevant statements from *Christianity*, *Other World Religions* and *Personal Search*. The exemplars go on to provide some background information for the teacher and an indication of the central themes relevant to personal search. Although aspects of the background information will feature in the 'finding out' stage of the process, ultimately, it will be for the teacher to decide how much of this is communicated to pupils. Also included is a list of the key words and concepts that pupils are likely to meet. Lastly some suggestions are made with regard to assessment.

The right-hand page consists of activities and questions arranged according to the process outlined in the associated reading. The first stage 'preparing the way' is omitted here because most of the activities relating to this stage will be repeated prior to every block of work or topic, for example, sharing targets, linking the new work to work already done, providing an overview of the content and activities to be covered, and generally trying to create a degree of interest and motivation. The activities and questions for discussion are arranged under the three remaining stages – 'finding out', 'making connections', and 'thinking it over'.

In summary the main elements of the exemplars are:

- title
- broad stage P1–P3/P4–P6/P7–S2
- targets
- key terms and concepts
- background information
- assessment.

The process

- Finding out
- Making connections
- Thinking it over

P1–P3

Title	**Birth of the Buddha**
Broad stage	P1–P3
Targets	Be familiar with stories associated with key figures (*Other World Religions*, Level B). Be able to share their ideas and feelings on ultimate questions (*Personal Search*, Level A).
Key terms and concepts	Buddha, Siddartha Gautama, monk, monastery, lotus flower, happiness, special, Hana Matsuri

Background information

Buddhism began in north east India around 450 BCE. It is based on the teachings of Siddhartha Gautama who became known as the Buddha, meaning 'enlightened one'. The Buddha taught that life is constantly changing and that happiness is not to be found in wealth, possessions or fame because these things eventually disappear. Instead we need to see the world as it really is and free ourselves from things like greed, selfishness and ignorance that keep us attached to the world as we would like it to be.

There are many myths and legends associated with the life of the Buddha. At his birth a wise man predicted that Siddartha would be a great and powerful leader. However, if he were once to see suffering of any kind he would give up his life of wealth and comfort to live a life of poverty as a holy man. In order to prevent this from happening his father tried to protect him from all the bad things in life. At the age of 29 he is said to have been confronted for the first time with illness, ageing and death. Soon after he decided to leave his home and devote himself to the search for truth and spiritual enlightenment.

For the life of the Buddha we rely almost entirely on the Buddhist scriptures preserved in a number of languages including Pali, Chinese and Tibetan. The teachings of the Buddha were passed on by monks, first by memory and then in written form. Today many Buddhists believe that only the life of the monk can prepare a person adequately to achieve enlightenment and so they try to spend some of their life in a monastery. In some Asian countries like Thailand and Burma, boys as young as eight are sent to monasteries to learn how to become Buddhist monks. Most of these young monks stay in the monastery for only a month or so before returning home. But some remain in the monastery and, at about the age of 20, are fully ordained as adult monks. Monks observe a strict way of life that involves having only a few basic possessions and being completely dependent on ordinary people for food, shelter and clothing. In return they teach and help the people.

Particularly in Japan the birth of the Buddha is celebrated at the festival of Hana Matsuri (the Festival of Flowers). It is said that the Buddha was born in a flower garden in the town of Lumbini in Nepal. In many homes therefore an image of the baby Buddha is placed on a stand in front of a miniature temple and decorated with flowers. Cherry blossom in particular is seen as a symbol of hope. The lotus flower is also used as a decoration and is a reminder of the Buddha's teaching. It is also seen as representing life and growing up. Its roots in the ground are like a baby beginning life. The flower rising is like a child growing up. When the petals start to open the flower is like someone who has learned to live at peace with everyone.

The personal search aspect of the exemplar focuses on discussing questions and issues relating to the themes of specialness, happiness and dreams.

Assessment

This will relate to the personal search target about sharing ideas and feelings on ultimate questions. Ask pupils to describe an occasion when they felt particularly happy. Is it possible to be happy all the time? Why or why not?

Finding out

Show pupils pictures of Buddhist monks or pictures of young boys training to be monks. What do they notice about them? What are they wearing? Why do you think they are dressed that way? Tell them about how young boys as young as eight spend some time in a monastery.

Talk about what life would be like as a monk especially the way they obtain their food, the difficulties of being away from home and what they might miss most. How would they feel if they were only allowed a very few clothes to wear? How would they feel if they had to depend on strangers for their food every day?

Tell them that in spending time as a monk the boys are following what the Buddha did a long time ago. The Buddha's real name was Siddartha Gautama. He is called the Buddha because he was a very special and holy person. Show pictures or artefacts of the Buddha. Pupils could be asked to imagine that they are about to visit someone really special. What would they do to prepare themselves? When they got there what would they want to say and do?

Read the story of the Buddha's birth. (Appendix 3 p. 71) Talk about the three main aspects of the story.
- Queen Maya has a strange dream – what was the dream about?
- A wise man said he was a very special baby – what made him think this?
- Siddartha's father did not want him to become a religious leader – how did his father try to prevent this happening?

Pupils could draw a picture of an aspect of the story and write (or have scribed for them) a sentence underneath to describe it.

Make a blossom tree by sticking pink and white tissue-paper flowers to twigs. Make a display of lotus-shaped flowers.

Making connections

Remind pupils about the signs on the baby Siddartha that made the wise man believe he was special. Ask pupils what physical characteristics/qualities/talents they have that make them special. Pupils could complete the sentence, 'I am special because ....' Is there any person you think is really special? What makes you think this?

Siddartha's father just wanted to make him happy? What makes you happy? Can people make us happy? How? Pupils could make two lists – the things that make them happy, people that make them happy. Pupils could bring in something that makes them happy – a favourite book, song or food.

What toys do you like playing with? Why are they your favourites? Pupils could draw a picture of their favourite toy and write a sentence underneath it saying why they like it?

What kind of things do you dream about? Write or draw about a dream you had recently.

Thinking it over

What was special about Siddhartha? Why do you think his father didn't want him to become a monk? Do you think he was right to keep him in the palace all the time? Why or why not? What makes someone special?

How do you know when you are happy? How do we know when other people are happy? Is it important to be happy? Is it possible to be happy all the time? What do you think we should do if we want to be happy? Do you have lots of toys and games? Do you think the more toys and games you have the happier you will be? Why or why not?

Do you often have dreams? Do you always remember your dreams? Why do you think this is? How do you know you are not dreaming now? Do dreams sometimes come true? Do you think we can learn anything from our dreams?

Title	**Christmas**
Broad stage	P1–P3
Targets	Be familiar with how Christmas is celebrated (*Christianity*, Level A).
	Be familiar with one of the stories of Jesus' birth (*Christianity*, Level A).
	Talk about ways in that people show care and concern (*Personal Search*, Level A).
Key terms and concepts	Jesus, angels, shepherds, manger, census, communication, caring.

Background information

The name Christmas comes from Christ's Mass (Eucharist or communion). In the early days of Christianity Easter was the main Christian festival. It was not until 400 years after the birth of Jesus that Christmas became an official day of celebration. Before that there were many mid-winter festivals in which people celebrated the fact that the worst of winter was over and warmer weather was on its way. The Romans for example had their festival of the sun on 25 December and the Anglo-Saxons had a winter festival about this time when the God Woden was celebrated.

Christians believe that God communicates with people and is intimately involved in the world he created. Underlying the Christian celebration of Christmas is the belief that Jesus is God's greatest communication. God sent Jesus into the world in order to bring people his message of love. Christians believe that Jesus was sent by God to show people how to live and to reveal to them what God was like.

This exemplar concentrates on that part of the Christmas story concerned with the journey to Bethlehem, the manger, and the role played by the angels and the shepherds in passing on the news about Jesus birth. In recent centuries the shepherds have became a popular Christian symbol. In Jesus' time, however, shepherds were often considered to be dishonest and untrustworthy. They frequently grazed their flocks on other people's land and, because of the nature of their job, were unable to attend the Temple worship like their fellow Jews. Nevertheless they are among the first to receive the angels' message. The story tells us that they were 'full of fear' when they saw the angels. Angel comes from a Greek word meaning messenger. In Christianity, and also in Judaism and Islam, angels act as intermediaries entrusted with divine messages for the world.

Luke tells us that Mary wrapped Jesus in strips of cloth and laid him in a manger, because there was no room for them at the inn. The Greek word for manger can mean a 'stall' for tying up animals or a 'manger' that is, a trough for feeding them. The picture of wrapping the baby and laying him down better supports the idea of a cradle-like manger. The details about being wrapped in strips of cloth and laid in a manger are clearly important because Luke repeats them again in relation to the shepherds. The shepherds are told that this is to be their sign.

The personal search aspect of the exemplar focuses on discussing questions and issues relating to the following themes – the importance of keeping in touch with people we know and love, and the need to show care and concern for others.

Assessment

This will relate to the personal search target about showing care and concern. Ask pupils to describe a situation when they showed care and concern. What did they do? Were they pleased with what they had done? Why?

Finding out

Read or tell Luke's story of the birth of Jesus. Ask pupils to listen carefully for the names of the people and places involved. Compile a list of the pupils' key words.

Begin discussion of the story by drawing out from pupils the contrasts between what they think is ordinary and what is special in the story. Pupils could then draw their favourite part of the story and write a sentence underneath to explain why. This could be the basis for making Christmas cards.

Ask the children how they could find out the number of pupils in the school. What else might they want to find out? – names, addresses, ages, gender, number of people in their family, occupations. Introduce the word 'census' – find out about the recent census – what is the purpose of a census? Tell the pupils that this is why Mary and Joseph had to go to Bethlehem – Joseph had to return to the place where he was born to be counted.

Talk about the journey from Nazareth to Bethlehem – use a map of modern day Israel to show pupils how far it is – How long would it take today by bus? How long would it have taken then? What means of transport would they have used then? What would they have had to take with them for the journey? How would they have been feeling about the baby's birth? Remind the pupils that eventually Mary and Joseph arrive in Bethlehem but are unable to find anywhere to stay.

Talk about the shepherds. How would they have felt when the angels appeared? – frightened? surprised? What might they have thought was happening? Who were these strange beings? What could they do with their sheep if they went to Bethlehem? Should they leave someone on guard? Tell pupils that:
- Christians believe Jesus was sent by God to show people how God wanted them to live
- this was the message the angels gave to the shepherds
- talk about the baby Jesus being wrapped in strips of cloth and laid in a manger. Why was Jesus wrapped in strips of cloth? Explain to pupils what a 'manger' is. Luke doesn't tell us exactly where Jesus was born. What do the pupils think?

The pupils could make puppets using paper plates, garden canes, card and wool. They could use the puppets to re-enact the journey to Bethlehem.

Making connections

Talk with pupils about the various ways we keep in touch with people – by telephone, letters, e-mail, talking. What are pupils' main forms of communication? Give pupils a short message to communicate and ask them to think of three different ways of doing this.

Pupils could talk to mums, dads, grandmas and grandads about how they prepared for the birth of their babies. Why do people print birth announcements in the newspapers? Can anyone bring in a copy of their own one?

Sometimes a baby is brought up by someone other than his/her own mother. Talk about adoption, care within extended families – emphasise that love and care are what matters most – link with Jesus being wrapped in strips of cloth. Show pictures and images of joy and trust eg a mother holding a baby, children playing with cuddly toys. Have the pupils held a new baby? How did they feel?

Make an 'All about Me' book of the first year of life bringing out the different people who were involved and who cared.

Thinking it over

What is the best way of keeping in touch with people you know? How often do you visit friends and relatives? Is it important to keep in touch with friends and relatives especially at Christmas? Why? What would happen if you didn't keep in touch with friends and relatives? Would that be a good thing or a bad thing? Why?

Mary cared for Jesus by wrapping him in strips of cloth. What other ways do parents care for their children? Do you think it is difficult to care for younger children? Why or why not? Do children get more difficult to care for as they get older? Why or why not? Is it just children who need care or do older people need to be cared for too? Why is it important to care for others? What can happen when people don't care?

Title	# Guru Nanak
Broad stage	P1–P3
Targets	Be familiar with stories associated with key figures (*Other World Religions*, Level B).
	Talk about people who help us and people we can help (*Personal Search*, Level A).
Key terms and concepts	Guru, turban, rupees, sharing, disagreements, service, quietness, meditation, God

Background information

The word 'Sikh' comes from Sanskrit language and means 'disciple'. Sikhs believe in one God and that everyone is equal, important and special. They were taught this by Guru Nanak who lived in the fifteenth century. Guru Nanak established the Sikh religion in the area of modern day Pakistan and north-west India, known as the Punjab. The fifteenth century was a time of great tension and conflict between Hindus and Muslims. Nanak believed that this was harmful to both Hindus and Muslims. He felt that both religions contained some of the truth about God but that their rituals were clouding the truth they were both trying to teach. The best way to find God he believed was to be still and meditate.

Sikhs believe that God created the world and all things in it but that God cannot himself be seen. He is invisible. As a result God made himself known through wise and holy teachers, or 'gurus'. Sikhism has ten gurus and Nanak was the first. Sikhism has a final guru in the form not of a person but a book, the Adi Granth (literally, the First Book). The book is a collection of the writings of the gurus and is honoured in the same way as the ten gurus. During worship members of the congregation must kneel in the presence of the Adi Granth and only approach it barefoot and with the head covered. On special occasions a member of the community or Granthi will lead the worship, waving a type of fan or whisk, called a chauri, over the text as he reads the words aloud.

Nanak believed that it was impossible to love God without also loving humanity, so he taught that people should be kind to one another and share what they have with others. Most of his teachings are contained in hymns and songs that are to be found in the Sikh scriptures. Pictures of Guru Nanak usually show him wearing the turban, which is the most distinctive feature of Sikh dress. It is formed from a long piece of cloth and is worn by men and boys and sometimes by girls particularly at festivals. Also present in pictures of the Guru is the central symbol of Sikhism, the 'Ek Aum Kar', which means 'there is one God'.

Most of the stories of Nanak's life are not contained in the Sikh scriptures but in collections of popular anecdotes. Some stories show his concern for the poor and needy such as the story of the Twenty Rupees a version of which can be found among the Appendices. Other stories tell of his miraculous powers and his outstanding wisdom and intellectual abilities. For Nanak, however, the important thing was how you behaved, how compassionate you were and what you did to bring about justice and a better society.

The personal search aspect of the exemplar focuses on discussing questions and issues relating to the themes of caring for others, agreement and disagreement and the importance of being quiet.

Assessment

This should relate to the personal search target about people who help us and people we can help. Ask pupils to describe a time when they helped someone. Do they think it is important to help people? Why?

Finding out

Look at pictures of Sikhs – draw pupils attention to the turban – tell pupils what it is, who wears it and why.

Prepare a template of the Sikh symbol, Ek Aum Kar, and get pupils to draw round it and cut it out on card – the symbol means one God

Tell pupils that Sikhs believe in one God and that everyone is important and special – they were told this by Guru Nanak, a religious teacher who lived in India many years ago.

Tell the story of Guru Nanak and the Twenty Rupees (Appendix 3 pp.71–72). Talk about the main aspects of the story.

- Nanak's father wants him to learn how to make money
- Nanak's meeting with the holy men
- The 20 rupees is spent on food
- His father's reaction

Pupils could draw a picture of Guru Nanak and all the food he bought for the holy men – they could write a sentence saying what they think of Guru Nanak

Pupils could find out about a local or famous individual who has helped others – why did he or she want to help others?

Find out about local organisations that set out to help people in the community. Invite someone from one of these organisations to tell pupils about the work they do.

Making connections

Nanak's father disagreed with what he did. Can you remember any disagreements you have had with people? What was the disagreement about? How did it get solved? How did you feel when you were quarrelling? Were you able to make up with the person with whom you were quarrelling? How did you feel about that?

Pupils could explore and express their ideas about quarrelling and making up through drawing, music and drama.

Nanak used to spend time on his own just being quiet and thinking about God. What is it like to be somewhere quiet? Have you ever been somewhere quiet? Where do you go to be quiet? Is it possible to be somewhere that is completely quiet? Why or why not?

Pupils could be given the opportunity to sit quietly, and then to note all the sounds they can pick up in the room, outside and in themselves.

Pupils could discuss the things they are expected to help with at home.

What things do we share in the classroom, in the school? Pupils could make two lists – one for the things shared in the classroom and one for things shared by the whole school.

What do you do to help others? Ask pupils about the reasons why they do things to help others as well as what they do. Are there times when they have done something to help others without being asked?

Thinking it over

Why do you think people are willing to spend time and energy helping people? Is it possible to help everyone who needs help? How do we decide who to help? Do you think we should help people we don't know? Why? Is it more important to help people we know than people we don't know? Why or why not?

Why do people sometimes quarrel? Are the causes of a quarrel always easy to put right? Why or why not? Is it important to try and make up after a quarrel? Why? Do you think people can learn not to quarrel? Do you think people can learn how to deal with quarrels once they start? Once a quarrel starts what do you think people should do to make sure it doesn't get worse?

Do you think it is a good idea to be quiet sometimes? Why do you think that? What are the times when you want to be quiet? Why do you want to be quiet then? Is it always easy to find a quiet place? Why not? Are there times when you wouldn't want to be quiet? Why?

Title	# Raksha Bandhan
Broad stage	P1–P3
Targets	Be familiar with how a major festival is celebrated and be able to describe associated customs (*Other World Religions*, Level A).
	Talk about some of the ways in which people show care and concern for others (*Personal Search*, Level A).
Key terms and concepts	Raksha, Bandhan, rakhi, caring, protection, Hindu, celebrating, festival, sari
Background information	In a Hindu family the male members have a duty to care and protect the female members. Even after the girl is married her brother continues to have a protective role, particularly if for some reason her husband is not there. This practice is celebrated each year during the month of August in the festival of Raksha Bandhan. Raksha means 'protection' and Bandhan means 'to tie'. At the festival sisters tie a 'rakhi' around their brother's wrist. It will often be made of red, gold or white silk but there are many variations. In return brothers give gifts to their sisters such as a sari, some money or sweets. The rakhi can also be placed around the wrist of another member of the family or a close friend who is regarded as a brother.
	Krishna is probably the most popular image of God for Hindus. His name means black or dark and images of him are usually dark in colour or blue. He is the eighth avatar or incarnation of the God Vishnu. Hindus believe that Vishnu comes into the world as an avatar when it is threatened by a crisis and can only be saved by divine intervention. He is the hero of the popular Hindu scripture known as the Bhagavad Gita.
	There are many stories about Krishna. Many tell of his miraculous birth. Others tell of his strength and courage as a child. He is said to have killed demons who threatened the children of his village and to have performed feats of amazing strength. Some stories talk about his lively and playful nature, showing him more as a normal child who was kind to others. One story, 'Krishna and his Two Sisters' is particularly associated with the festival of Raksha Bandhan. Krishna's two sisters were very different from one another. Subhadra, his real sister, was always grumbling and complaining especially about Draupadi, Krishna's adopted sister. Subhadra was jealous of Draupadi and thought that Krishna paid more attention to Draupadi than to her. When one day Krishna cut his hand it was Draupadi who looked after him and bandaged his hand.
	The personal search aspect of the exemplar focuses on discussing questions and issues relating to the themes of family, getting on with others and the importance of giving.
Assessment	This should relate to the personal search target about showing care and concern for others. Ask pupils to describe a time when they gave a gift to someone special. What was the gift? Who was it for and what was the occasion? Why is it important to give gifts?

Finding out

Read or tell the story of 'Krishna and his two sisters' (Appendix 3 p. 73). Tell the pupils that Krishna is a very special person to Hindus and there are many stories about how kind he was and how he liked to help people.

Talk about the main aspects of the story. For example:
- the relationship between Krishna and his two sisters Subhadra and Draupadi
- Subhadra's reaction when Krishna cuts his hand
- the reaction of Druapada.

Pupils could draw a picture of what happened when Krishna cuts his hand showing how one of the sisters reacted. They could write a sentence under it saying who they thought was the best sister to Krishna and why.

Tell pupils that Hindu boys and girls remember this story today at the festival of Raksha Bandhan in August – tell them what each of the words means and explain how the festival is celebrated. Talk about the words 'celebration' and 'festival' – what do they mean? what kind of events do people celebrate? Birthdays, weddings, christenings? Who shares in these celebrations? What preparations are necessary? Why do people celebrate?

Make wrist bands by plaiting wool or ribbon together.

Discuss who pupils might want to present with a rakhi, relation, friend, neighbour – why would they choose that person?

Pupils could get involved in making Indian sweets from sugar, water, dried milk and desiccated coconut.

Making connections

Talk about the relationships between brothers and sisters – what makes them special?

The two sisters in the story did not get on – Do you get on with your brothers and sisters? Are there things about them that annoy you? Are there things about you that annoy them? What do you do to show you care for them? Have you ever really needed your big brother/sister's help for something? When? What happened?

Ask pupils to think of an occasion when they have cared for and protected someone.

Working together in groups pupils could decide on a few objects that make them feel safe, protected and cared for – they could make a display and include the reasons why.

Talk about why pupils might need protection and how they might protect others

Pupils could think of ways in which to make their class/school a safer and more caring place and how they could be more caring and protective to others.

At the festival of Raksha Bandhan the sister gives her brother/cousin/friend a rakhi and the brother gives her a gift of some sort – Do you get excited when you get a gift? Why? On what occasions do we usually give gifts? Whom have you given a gift to recently?

Thinking it over

Is it always easy to love and care for brothers and sisters? Why or why not? Are there times when it is difficult? Can you give any examples? What is the difference between family and friends?

What should we do if we do not like someone but we meet them everyday? What can we do if we think someone doesn't like us? Is it possible to get on well with everybody? Should we try?

Is it important to give presents/gifts to people you love? Why? How else could you show you care for them? Is it important to always buy an expensive gift? Why or why not? What do people mean when they say 'it's the thought that counts'? Do you agree?

P4–P6

Title	# Ceremonies in Hinduism – beginning the journey of life
Broad stage	P4–P6
Targets	Know what happens in a birth ceremony (*Other World Religions*, Level B).
	Be able to explain the symbolism involved in a birth ceremony (*Other World Religions*, Level C).
	Reflect with support on the natural order of the animal and human life-cycle – birth, growth – in association with religious ceremonies marking these stages (*Personal Search*, Level C).
Key terms and concepts	Samskaras, ceremony, the aum symbol, identity, stages in life, life as a journey
Background information	Many religions teach that life is like a journey. In Hinduism there are a number of ceremonies (samskaras) that mark different stages in the journey of life, life from pre birth to death. There are 16 such samskaras though not all are commonly performed today. The most common ones relate to pre-birth, the day of birth, naming, and growing up.

Pre-Birth: At some time during the pregnancy of the mother, the family will get together for a celebration meal and say prayers for the safe arrival of the baby.

Day of Birth: After washing the baby, the main custom on the day of birth is placing honey on the baby's tongue and tracing the symbol 'Aum' on the baby's tongue. Aum for Hindus is a sacred symbol. It might be said to represent God. Honey represents sweetness. It is hoped that the child will have a sweet, good life free from illness and the bad things of the world, and also that the child might have a sweet nature. Prayers will be said. For example the father might say 'Oh dear child, I give you this honey that has been provided by God who is the producer of all the wealth of the world – may you be preserved and protected by God and live in this world for 100 autumns.'

Naming: The naming ceremony takes place about 10 or 12 days after the birth. The name is usually chosen by the family, often after advice from a Hindu priest. He will prepare a horoscope for the child and perhaps suggest a letter from the alphabet for the initial letter for the name of the child. Children are often named after a Hindu deity. The child will be dressed in a new garment and placed in a swinging cot surrounded by diva lamps. The lamps give light and warmth. The whole atmosphere suggests a happy, warm, secure environment surrounded by light. This symbolises that what children need most of all is a secure environment. It is a day of joy and celebration and gifts will be brought for the child. The gift may include something that the child can keep for the rest of their life such as gold jewellery.

Growing up: There are a number of ceremonies to mark important stages as a child develops and grows up. These include the child's first outing, first solid food and first haircut. At about 4 months there is a ritual outing. The child at sunrise is bathed and dressed in new clothes and taken out to see the sun and feel its warmth. Later the family and the child will go to the local temple. At about 6 months a ceremony marks the first solid food eaten by the child. The food will be a mouthful of something like cooked rice with honey and yoghurt. The ceremony in which the head is shaven is usually for boys only. This ceremony happens after a boy is 1 and before he is 5. Removing hair is a sign of cleansing and Hindus believe that in doing this bad deeds from a previous life are removed.

The personal search aspect of the exemplar focuses on discussing questions and issues relating to the themes of family life, family celebrations and stages in life.

Assessment	This will relate to the personal search target about reflecting on the human life-cycle and associated religious ceremonies. Ask pupils to say what they think are the main stages of life. Which of the above ceremonies do they think are the most important and why?

Finding out

Teachers might 'invent' a Hindu family for pupils to explore. This Hindu family might be given names such as Mr and Mrs Datta. The story of the family would tell of the birth and the early life of a child.

Pupils might share their experiences about the birth of a younger sibling and have visits to the classroom from a mother with a young baby to talk about important stages in a child's development.

Build up a frieze showing the various ceremonies involved. Discuss feelings experienced by the family at each ceremony.

In relation to specific ceremonies:

*   *Pre-birth* – discuss what 'safe arrival' means. Pupils could make up a simple prayer asking for a safe arrival.

*   *Day of birth* – pupils could draw the Aum symbol. They could taste some Hindu sweets. Discuss with pupils what it means to have a sweet life, and consider the contrast between having a sweet and a sour nature.

*   *Naming* – talk about the reasons for symbols such as diva lamps and a rocking cradle. Tell pupils a prayer, e.g. 'May God the creator of all good things grant you wisdom' and identify what is wished for. Pupils could role play the naming ceremony.

*   *Growing up* – pupils could develop a time line of the stages in a Hindu's child's early years, drawing a picture to represent each samskara.

Making connections

Helps pupils identify cycles in the natural world and in life. Discuss how life is a series of beginnings and endings. Identify different ways the birth of a baby is celebrated. Discuss with pupils times they have been present at a birth ceremony.

Pupils could talk about their life so far and draw a time line of important events and achievements. Organise a display of memorabilia to represent their life so far.

Help pupils think about the future. What important decisions about the future have to be made? Discuss with pupils what it means to say 'life is like a journey'.

In relation to specific ceremonies:

*   *Pre-birth* – pupils could suggest feelings a family might have when hearing that a baby is expected. They could identify what has to be done to prepare for the arrival of the baby.
*   *Day of birth* – pupils could talk about times they have shown a sweet nature and a sour nature. They could design a welcoming baby card that contains wishes and hopes for a baby.
*   *Naming* – discuss why it is important to have a name. Organise a survey to find out the popular names in the school. Pupils could play a game by being given a letter of the alphabet and thinking of as many names as possible.
*   *Growing up* – look at baby books to identify significant moments. Pupils could think about how they have changed and developed by completing the sentence ' three years ago I could not ... but now I can ...' in as many different ways as possible.

Thinking it over

What is a family? What different kinds of families are there? Why are they important? In what ways has your family influenced you? How do you feel about that? What contribution do you make to family life? Could you do more?

Is it a good idea for families to celebrate together? Do celebrations always strengthen family life? What makes you think that? Is it important to have family celebrations that mark particular stages in life? Why or why not? What have you achieved recently that is worthy of celebration?

What different stages are there in life? What is your next big stage in life? How can you prepare for it? Are you looking forward to it? Why or why not? What do you hope for the future – for yourself, your family, the world? What kind of person do you want to be?

Title	**The Sangha**
Broad stage	P4–P6
Targets	To understand the significance of customs associated with Buddhism, e.g. the way Buddhist monks/nuns dress, their attitude to food, etc. (*Other World Religions*, Level C). Show some knowledge and understanding of the code of conduct in Buddhism, e.g. the 10 precepts (*Other World Religions*, Level C). Reflect on the benefits and responsibilities of belonging to groups (*Personal Search*, Level C) to appreciate the need for rules (*Personal Search*, Level C).
Key terms and concepts	Sangha, precepts, meditation, community, rules, commitment, lifestyle.
Background information	An important statement in Buddhism is the three refuges. It is a statement of commitment in the form of a prayer. The statement is 'I go for refuge to the Buddha; I go for refuge to the Dharma; I go to for refuge to the Sangha'. Buddhists therefore turn to the Buddha, the enlightened one, the Dharma, the teachings of the Buddha, and the Sangha, the Buddhist Community. Sangha refers to the monastic community (monks and nuns), who set an example to all Buddhists. Some of the early followers of the Buddha, gave up family life to spend time travelling around with the Buddha. They were the first monks. Other followers stayed at home and supported the travelling monks by giving food, etc. They were the lay people. Today there are Buddhist monasteries throughout the world. According to Buddhist teaching, the life of a monk should be as simple as possible to avoid distraction from spiritual tasks. Life in a Buddhist monastery is hard and also strict. The monks are not allowed to work for money or to cook their own food. There are precise instructions about every aspect of the monk's religious life. Monks are expected to keep 10 precepts or rules, the first five of which are for all Buddhists. The first five are – to abstain from harming living things, taking that which is not given, sexual misconduct (in primary school this might be explored as not being greedy), false speech (not to say unkind things or tell lies), drugs or drink that cloud the mind. Monks and nuns try to practise a further five precepts – to abstain from eating after midday, jewellery, perfumes and garlands, entertainments, a luxurious bed, handling gold or silver. They are expected to beg for their food and are allowed only a few possessions – a robe, an alms bowl, a water filter, a razor and a needle. Life in the monastery consists mostly of meditation, the study of the scriptures and participation in religious ceremonies. Monks usually go out into the community and, in return for gifts of food and clothing, provide spiritual guidance. In this topic pupils might explore the lifestyle and commitment of Buddhist monks and nuns through looking especially at the possessions of a monk, the 10 rules or precepts monks keep, and how monks spend their time in a monastery (see Appendix 4 p. 73). The personal search aspect of the exemplar focuses on discussing questions and issues relating to the themes of possessions, rules and commitment.
Assessment	This could relate to the personal search target about the benefits and responsibilities of belonging to groups. Pupils could complete a number of sentences such as: • one thing I admire about Buddhist monks/nuns is … because … • one thing I would like about living in a Buddhist community is … • I couldn't live like a Buddhist monk/nun because … • Showing commitment to a group/community I belong to involves ….

Finding out

As the topic proceeds pupils could build up a frieze showing the lifestyle and activities of monks/nuns.

Show pupils a poster of Buddhists monks/nuns collecting for food. What do they see? What is a monk/nun? Why are they given food? Tell pupils about the possessions of a monk/nun and discuss why each is needed.

For example *the robe* can lead to a discussion about the impact of fashion/designer clothes in today's world and/or a discussion about dressing in a uniform way; *the alms bowl* can be used to help pupils reflect on the ways people are dependent on each other; *the water filter* might lead to a discussion of not harming any creature, including the smallest; *the needle* is for mending a robe instead of replacing it. Pupils might discuss this in the context of today's 'throw away society'; *the razor* is used to shave hair as a sign of modesty and giving up self pride. Pupils might discuss what modesty and self pride mean and which is more important how a person looks or how a person lives.

Pupils could find out about the 10 precepts and discuss what each teaches about belief and lifestyle. Are they easy to keep? Which is the most important? Pupils could try to write some of the precepts in a positive way.

Tell pupils about a typical day in the life of a Buddhist monk/nun. Pupils could draw pictures to represent the different activities in the day. They could discuss what aspects of a typical day they like and don't like.

Making connections

Pupils could talk about communities they belong to. Why do they go? What communities do they have to belong to? Which do they choose to belong to? What do they enjoy doing? What do they dislike? Are there any rules? What responsibilities do they have? Do they feel committed? A wall display of the communities they belong to could be produced.

Pupils could draw their own favourite possessions and identify five they think they could not live without. They could survey friends and family to find out their most precious possessions and discuss the results. A class discussion about the difference between things we need and things we desire could be held. Pupils might discuss the relevance of the possessions of a Buddhist monk/nun for today.

Pupils could talk about why rules are necessary. They could identify rules that would make the classroom a happy place, where learning can take place. These could be displayed. They could give their ideas about rules that would make the world a better place.

Pupils could write a diary extract of a typical pupil day, and identify ways in which their day is similar to and different from a Buddhist monk. Pupils could discuss why Buddhists spend time meditating. What do pupils do and where do they go when they want to be quiet and thoughtful? Pupils might discuss and plan how a corner in the classroom might be used as a quiet place.

Thinking it over

Do you think the more possessions we have the happier we will be? Why or why not? What do you think makes people happy? What makes you happy? Possessions don't always last – they break or become obsolete. What might we want to last for ever (for example love, friendship, security)? Which is more important, what people own or how they live their lives? What makes you think that? What do you value most in life?

Why are rules important? What would it be like if there were no rules? Should rules always be obeyed? Why or why not? If there was to be only one rule for living what would it be?

Buddhist monks are committed to a certain way of life. What does it mean to be committed to something or someone, for example a cause, an ideal, certain beliefs? Is it important to be committed to something like this? Why or why not? Could you commit yourself to the lifestyle of a Buddhist monk? With which aspects of that lifestyle would you have most difficulty?

Title	# A visit to a Church of Scotland parish church
Broad stage	P4–P6
Targets	Be aware of local churches and their association with Sunday worship and special occasions such as baptisms (*Christianity*, Level B). Show some knowledge and understanding of the design and furnishings of churches and of the worship that takes place there (*Christianity*, Level C). Develop the confidence and ability to express their own questions … in response to their awareness of religion (*Personal Search*, Level B).
Key terms and concepts	Words connected with the main features of a church building such as pulpit, font, table for Holy Communion and the concepts of worship, respect, community, belonging.
Background information	This exemplar focuses on a visit by pupils to explore a local Church of Scotland church. It is important to allow pupils to identify lines of interest and inquiry themselves. During the visit it would be helpful if Christians from the church (minister and lay people) were on hand to respond to queries and explain why the church is important to them, and later were invited to the school to view follow up work and engage in further dialogue. Pupils might explore why Christians go to church, what Christians do when they go to church, and why the building is special for them. The First Book of Discipline of the Church of Scotland states, 'Every Church must have a pulpit, a basin for baptism and a table for the ministration of the Lord's Supper.' Preaching the word, baptism and communion are the key elements of the Reformed Church and these are the aspects that might be specifically looked at. Listening to the 'Word of God' read from the Bible is an important part of every service in the Reformed Church. The Bible is not one book but a whole library of books. It is divided into two main sections, the Old Testament and the New testament. In the New Testament the four gospels are particularly important because they are about the life of Jesus. Christians look on the Bible as a guide to what they should believe and how they should live. Some take the Bible literally and follow its teachings without question. Others interpret the Bible in the light of modern developments and their own consciences. Baptism marks admission to the Christian Church. It recalls the moment, when Jesus was baptised by John the Baptist in the waters of the River Jordan. Communion commemorates the Last Supper when Jesus told his disciples to eat bread (his body) and drink wine (his blood) in remembrance of him. For Christians, attending a church for worship involves a variety of feelings such as thankfulness, humility, joy at being with other Christians. Pupils might be encouraged to find out why Christians have these feelings, and reflect on occasions when they have had similar feelings. Pupils might also engage in ideas about the atmosphere found in a church building. Visiting a church and meeting with Christians should also help pupils to appreciate the importance of listening to what they have to say and of showing respect for the beliefs and practices of believers. The personal search aspect of the exemplar focuses on discussing questions and issues relating to the themes of respect, belonging and the importance of listening.
Assessment	This will relate to the personal search target about developing the confidence and ability to express their own questions. Pupils could be asked to make a list of the questions raised by their visit to the church and to put them in order of importance.

Finding out

Before the visit: pupils could identify important buildings in their community. Why do people go? What are the important features? Show pupils photographs/video of a church. Pupils could suggests reasons why Christians go, and identify important features. Use the photographs/video to introduce pupils to the concept of worship and discuss how and why Christians worship. Prepare for a visit by discussing how respect can be shown on the visit.

During the visit: Using a structured worksheet, pupils could explore key features especially the pulpit, the font and the communion table. They could take photographs of and draw key features. They could ask questions to find out why these features are important to Christians. They could ask Christians what going to Church means to them and record responses. They could collect Church magazines to find out more about the life of the church.

After the visit: Pupils could build up a class book of their visit, focusing especially on worship in the church. It could include a list of people involved in the life of the church; activities that go on in the church; different ways the church is involved in the community; a series of word bubbles explaining why the Church is important to Christians. Pupils could discuss how Christians show respect for the church, and why Christians believe belonging to a church is like belonging to a family.

Making connections

Before a visit: Pupils could identify a place special to them. Why do they go there? What makes it special? How is it respected? From their experience pupils could discuss how buildings/places can evoke feelings and talk about peaceful, scary, comforting, happy places, etc. They might discuss how a building such as an airport can be a happy place, a sad place, an exciting place, etc. A visitor might talk about a special place for them that evokes feelings and memories. Pupils could talk about times they have been to a church. Why did they go? What was it like?

During a visit: Pupils might experience a time of stillness and quiet reflection; listen to the organ, the church bell, a prayer, a reading from the Bible. Pupils could identify words to describe the atmosphere of the church, and discuss occasions they have experienced similar feelings.

After a visit: Pupils could discuss why Christians find it helpful to meet with other Christians and relate this to their own experiences of being with others. They could relate reasons Christians go to church to their own ideas and experiences. For example, Christians go to church for comfort and encouragement. Who do pupils turn to for encouragement and comfort? Christians go to church to give thanks to God. Who do pupils give thanks to? What for? How?

Thinking it over

What makes a building special? Do you have a special place you like to go to? Is it important for you to have a special place? Why? How do you expect people to treat your special place? What is respect? In what kinds of places do people show respect? Why? How is respect shown? Is there a particular person whom you have great respect for? What is it about that person that makes you feel this way?

What groups do you belong to? What benefits do you think there are in belonging to a group? What problems can arise within a group? Can these problems always be resolved? Christians believe that belonging to a church is like belonging to a family. In what ways might a church be like a family? Do Christians really need a special building to meet in? Why or why not?

Is it always easy to listen to what others are saying? Why not? What can get in the way? Is it sometimes important to listen to what other have to say? Why? If we listen do we always have to accept what is said? Why or why not? Christians try to listen to what is said in the Bible? In what ways might this be helpful to Christians? Is there something or someone to whom you try to listen?

Title	**Zakah and Muslim aid**
Broad stage	P4–P6
Targets	Show some knowledge and understanding of the code of conduct in Islam, the 'five Pillars of Islam' (*Other World Religions*, Level C). Recognise that religion is essentially about ultimate questions (*Personal Search*, Level C). Show awareness of and concern for the needs of groups in society through the work of specific charities (*Personal Search*, Level D).
Key terms and concepts	The five Pillars, Zakah, duty, giving, charity, generosity, selfishness
Background information	Just as the pillars in a mosque support the building that rises above them, so the Pillars of Islam support the beliefs of the Islamic faith. The five Pillars of Islam are: • the Shahada – the basic statement of faith, i.e. 'There is no God but Allah and Muhammad is the messenger of Allah' • Salat – daily worship, the prayers that are recited five times a day, at dawn, midday, afternoon, evening and night • Sawm – fasting that involves going without food and drink during daylight hours throughout the holy month of Ramadan • Hajj – pilgrimage, that all healthy Muslim men and women are expected to make at least once in a lifetime • Zakah – charitable giving. It refers to using money/wealth to help those in need. It is a duty that Muslims should fulfil and not a voluntary activity. In addition many Muslims do give money voluntarily (Sadaquah) to people in need. Muslims believe that everything on this earth belongs to Allah. Helping people through giving is a way of submitting to the will of Allah. For Muslims Zakah enables the poor as well as the rich to have a claim on wealth and so there is no shame in receiving Zakah. Zakah for the giver is a way of removing feelings of selfishness and greed. In this way it is said to purify an individual's wealth. Each year (often at the end of Ramadan) Muslims will work out how much Zakah has to be paid and make arrangements to pay it. How much is paid depends on the wealth of a Muslim. Muslims pay 2.5 per cent of their wealth each year to Zakah. The money might be given to a local mosque to help those in need in the local community or it might be given to an organisation such as Muslim Aid. Muslim Aid aims to help those who are suffering because of poverty, war and natural disaster throughout the world. The personal search aspect of the exemplar focuses on discussing questions and issues relating to the themes of giving, selfishness and duty.
Assessment	Pupils could write a newspaper article for a magazine that informs non-muslims about the Muslim duty of Zakah. Pupils would set out the article in the form of a newspaper with an appropriate heading , and possibly an advert for Muslim aid. In addition pupils might write an opinion column article under the heading 'Should we help people in need?' This would enable the teacher to assess pupils' knowledge and understanding of Zakah and their awareness and concern for the needs of groups in society.

Finding out

Tell pupils part of the story of the two brothers (see Appendix 4 p. 74). Ask pupils to predict the ending. Discuss what the story teaches about giving , generosity and caring.

Pupils could find out what is meant by Zakah and the rules of Zakah, and record their findings. They could produce a poster headed 'Zakah' to illustrate what Zakah is about.

They could be given a number of simple scenarios describing the wealth of a Muslim family and work out, using a calculator, how much a family would pay in Zakah. Pupils could discuss why Zakah is a duty for Muslims.

Tell pupils a saying of Muhammad (see Appendix 4 p. 74) and discuss what it teaches about charity. Pupils could write their own poem explaining how actions can be charity.

Give pupils a hand out describing the work of Muslim Aid (see Appendix 4 p. 74). Pupils, using the Muslim Aid web site, could find out where and how Zakah money is used in the world today. Pupils could create a frieze showing how Muslim Aid helps people.

They could discuss the meaning of the Muslim Aid slogan 'Working together for others' and whether it is an effective slogan. They could represent this slogan in a pictorial way with drawings and/or cut outs from magazines or make up their own slogan. They could imagine they live in a place where water was obtained from a well two miles away until Muslim Aid came and provided water, and write an account of the change it made to their lives.

Pupils could research a charity to find out what the charity does, listen to a visitor from the charity, plan a fund raising event to raise money for the charity and identify ways (other than giving money) of supporting the charity.

Making connections

Pupils could discuss from their own experiences the meaning of the words 'generosity' and 'selfishness'. They could explain how they feel when someone is generous or selfish to them. They could identify ways of being generous, other than giving money. They could make up and act out a drama to illustrate generosity.

Explore with pupils their own approach to giving to charity. Have they been involved in a class project for charity? Do they give to charity? When? What charities do they give to? Who do these charities help?

Display a list of charities pupils have supported with a brief description of the work of the charities. Identify different 'charity shops' and make a visit to one to find out what it does and how people use their time to help the charity by actions. Pupils could discuss occasions when they have done charitable actions.

Thinking it over

Should we give to charity? How do we decide which charity to give to? If we give to charity should we tell others? Should we give on a regular basis or just when we feel like it? Does it always help to give money? Why or why not? It is more rewarding to give than to receive. Do you agree? Some say charity begins at home. What do you think?

Zakah is a duty. What does it means to 'do your duty'? What duties might we have to our family and friends? Do we have a duty to be concerned about people in need? Do we have a duty to help people even if they live a long way away in another country? Should it be compulsory to help people in need? Are we free to do just as we want? Why or why not?

Why are people sometimes selfish? What I do with my money is my own affair and nothing to do with anyone else. Do you agree? Muslims believe that no one has a right to live in luxury while others go hungry? Do you agree?

P7–S2

Title	# The Sikh Langar
Broad stage	P7–S2
Targets	Show some understanding of central principles in Sikhism, e.g. sewa and equality (*Other World Religions*, Level D). Show some understanding of general moral principles (*Personal Search*, Level D). Be able to identify, discuss and apply such principles in real situations, e.g. the principle of equality (*Personal Search*, Level D). Be able to express informed opinions about how beliefs are applied to social and moral issues (*Other World Religions*, Level E).
Key terms and concepts	Langar, gurdwara, sewa, vand chhakna, welcoming, hospitality, fairness, justice, equality
Background information	The Sikh religion was founded in the fifteenth century by Guru Nanak. It was a time of great tension in the Punjab between Hindus and Muslims and Guru Nanak believed that a new way forward had to be found. 'There is neither Hindu nor Muslim', he said, 'so whose path shall I follow.' Nanak believed that loving God was impossible without loving humanity, so he taught that people should be kind to their neighbours and share what they had with those less fortunate than themselves. The langar or shared dining room is therefore an important feature of every temple or gurdwara. It is the communal kitchen and serves vegetarian food. For Sikhs it expresses the importance of one of the key principles of Sikhism – sewa or service. In the langar Sikhs demonstrate service to others by preparing, cooking and distributing food. It also demonstrates the principle 'Vand Chhakna', sharing of earnings. Sikhs will use their money to buy the food to be served and shared with others. The langar is open to all, regardless of religion, social class, wealth, gender, and so emphasises the Sikh belief in the equality of humanity. The Gurus rejected the caste system. They welcomed people of all religions and they rejected social distinctions caused by wealth. For Sikhs, eating together breaks down barriers and is a basic principle of the langar. This is demonstrated in the saying of one of the Gurus 'first eat together then we'll talk together'. In the Guru Granth Sahib and the Rehat Maryada (a guide to the Sikh way of life) can be found many sayings that emphasis the importance of equality for Sikhs, for example: • 'He is religious who regards all men as equal.' (Guru Nanak) • 'Know that all mankind is one caste' (Guru Gobind Singh) • 'From the Divine Light the whole creation sprang why then should we divide creatures into high and low.' (Guru Granth Sahib) • 'A gurdwara is open to anyone regardless of caste or creed.' (Rehat Maryada) • 'In the congregation there should be no distinction of social status or caste or between Sikh and non-Sikh' (Rehat Maryada) • 'Sitting on special cushions, chairs, couches or sofas or in any other way demonstrating social distinction or superiority is deemed contrary to Sikhism.' (Rehat Maryada) • 'There should be no privileged seating, or priority in feeding people in the langar … .The emphasis should be on brotherhood.' (Rehat Maryada). The personal search aspect of the exemplar focuses on discussing questions and issues relating to the themes of hospitality, service, justice and equality.
Assessment	At Level D, pupils are expected to be able 'to discuss and apply the principle of equality'. Teachers could present pupils with a moral dilemma situation so that they could listen to groups engaged in discussion. Pupils would be asked to explain the dilemma relating to equality/inequality and how they would resolve it.

Finding out

Using a thesaurus, pupils could find out the meaning of the word 'hospitality'. They could find out what goes on in a langar and explain how and why the langar demonstrates hospitality. If possible a visit to a langar to experience hospitality should be arranged. Pupils could write a letter expressing thanks for the hospitality. They could devise a poster inviting and welcoming all to the langar, using appropriate words and Sikh symbols.

Pupils could discuss what it means to serve others. They could identify all the jobs that need to be done to prepare, serve and clear up a meal in the langar. They could devise a series of cartoon pictures with captions under the heading ' my day at the langar serving others' or write a description of serving in the langar in the style of 'a day in the life of ...'.

Discuss with pupils what being involved in the langar teaches about sewa, vand chhakna and use of time. Pupils could plan a vegetarian meal and work out the cost in terms of money and time.

Pupils could research the caste system and explain the opposition of the Gurus to it.

They could examine quotes from the Sikh Scripture and the Rehat Maryada about equality and discuss what each teaches. They could rewrite some of the quotes using modern terminology and produce a collage of quotes, accompanied by appropriate pictures. Pupils could explore the Sikh saying 'In Sikhism there is no Muslim or Hindu, beggar or emperor, priest or untouchable – all are equal in God's eyes' and write their own version for today's society.

Making connections

Talk with pupils about times they have received and shown hospitality; how they felt when going somewhere new for the first time and how being welcomed can help; what the characteristics of a good welcome are. Visitors might be invited to the class (perhaps Sikhs from a local gurdwara) and a welcome prepared for them.

Talk with pupils about their experiences of serving others – when, how, why, how did people respond, how did they feel. Pupils could write an account of one such time.

Pupils could identify the skills and abilities they have that could be used to help others. A class list of skills could be produced.

Pupils could produce a number of 'It's not fair' statements based on their own experiences and their knowledge of the national/world scene. Pupils might put them in order of 'unfairness'.

Pupils could discuss examples of equality/inequality at home/school/the workplace/the wider world. They could share their understanding, of the statement 'all humans are born free and equal'.

Thinking it over

Is it important to show hospitality? Why or why not? Who should hospitality be shown to? Should we show hospitality to everyone who knocks on our door? Is the UK an hospitable or inhospitable country today? What makes you think this? Can people take advantage of hospitality?

Is it important that people serve others? Do we have a responsibility for other people? Why or why not? How do we decide who to serve? Can serving others sometimes be done for selfish reasons? Which is harder to give, money or time?

Is the world a fair and just place? What makes you think this? Is our school/local community a fair and just place? Who is to blame if there is inequality in society? Is inequality a good thing or a bad thing? Should everybody be treated equally? Why or why not? Does treating people equally mean treating them in the same way? What could be done to promote greater equality?

Title	**Yom Kippur and the story of Jonah**
Broad stage	P7–S2
Targets	Show some understanding of the connection between customs and beliefs (*Other World Religions*, Level E).
	Understand the significance of a festival (Yom Kippur) by investigating the key beliefs associated with it (*Other World Religions*, Level F).
	Understand that for many people religious beliefs provide a sense of meaning and purpose in life (*Personal Search*, Level E).
Key terms and concepts	Yom Kippur, forgiveness, repentance, confession, sin, evil, atonement, meaning and purpose.
Background information	The Jewish New Year begins with Rosh Hashanah. This is a time when Jews look back on mistakes they have made during the previous year and resolve to do better in the year to come. A ram's horn, called a shofar, is blown to call all sinners to repentance. The Rosh Hashanah festival commemorates God's creation and is a reminder that everything we do will be judged. Traditionally, Jews eat apples dipped in honey and wish each other a 'sweet' new year. The next ten days are called the Days of Penitence and are spent reflecting and preparing for Yom Kippur, the most sacred day of the religious calendar.

At Yom Kippur Jews confess their sins and pray for forgiveness. It is a solemn day. However, it is not a day of sadness because for Jews there is a sense of confidence in God's forgiveness and in the ability of human beings to assess their actions and improve themselves. An important custom on the eve of Yom Kippur is for Jews to ask forgiveness of each other for any wrongs they may have committed or any pain they have caused. Yom Kippur itself is a day of fasting for all adults who are healthy. Fasting is a way of showing that the desire for forgiveness is genuine. The day will be spent in the synagogue in prayer, and listening to readings from the Torah. These will include the reading from Leviticus telling of the ancient atonement ritual involving a scapegoat to bear away sins. The parable of Jonah is also read, because it teaches Jews about God's infinite capacity to forgive all mankind, even those who are thought not to deserve forgiveness. For Jews it is a lesson of God's desire to help rather than punish.

To help pupils explore forgiveness, teachers might find a case study from a newspaper or a television programme that illustrates some one prepared to show forgiveness. Recently a headline in a national newspaper was 'Widow prays for a freed IRA gunman'. This was an account of how a widow was hoping that the killer of her husband would make a success of his life on leaving prison. Pupils might read and discuss a similar case study and give a personal response to it. Pupils might be able to identify similar case studies and stories about forgiveness that could be shared and discussed.

The personal search aspect of the exemplar focuses on discussing questions and issues relating to the themes of forgiveness, taking stock and the nature of evil. |
| Assessment | Assessment could focus on the two Level E targets. Pupils could produce a mind/concept map showing how and why Jews celebrate Yom Kippur. They could explain how certain beliefs about forgiveness can contribute to people's sense of meaning and purpose in life. |

Finding out

Tell the story 'Blowing in the wind' (Appendix 5 p. 75) and discuss with pupils what it teaches about relationships, saying sorry and forgiveness.

Pupils could use books and the internet to research and present a group report on 'when, how and why Jews observe Yom Kippur'. They could include a glossary of key terms, explaining the meaning of sin, confession, forgiveness and repentance.

Pupils could write a diary extract imagining they attended a Yom Kippur observance, explaining what they did and how they felt. They could respond to the Yom Kippur saying, 'A person should make up with his friend the day before Yom Kippur' by devising a poster on the theme 'a time for making up'. In groups, they could write a short article for a Jewish magazine headed 'Why it is important for Jews today to observe Yom Kippur'.

Tell pupils the story of the scapegoat (see Appendix 5 p. 75) and discuss its teaching.

Read an abridged version of the parable of Jonah. Pupils could be given the story in sections and devise their own heading for each section. They could discuss the story in groups and explain why it is an appropriate story for Yom Kippur. They could write a short dialogue between Jonah and God with Jonah giving reasons why he didn't want to go to Nineveh, and God explaining why he must.

Making connections

Discuss with pupils the different ways it is possible to 'hurt' someone. Pupils could identify times they have 'hurt' someone and said sorry, and times when someone has 'hurt' them and said sorry. They could explore feelings involved in saying sorry and identify different reactions to being 'hurt' such as bearing a grudge, taking revenge, making up, making recompense.

They could devise a role play to illustrate different responses to a given scenario such as gossiping, breaking a promise. In response to the story 'Blowing in the wind' they could write their own story based on their experiences ending with the words 'It's hard to clean up'.

Jews assess their lives at Yom Kippur. Pupils might discuss what is involved in a successful life. They could reflect on their own lives and identify:

- three things they have done in the last year they are sorry for
- three steps they could take to improve a relationship with a parent or friend
- three good qualities they have
- three aspects of their character they might try to change.

Pupils could look at a case study of an example of forgiveness in today's world and give their own views on what happened.

Thinking it over

Is it easy to admit you are in the wrong and say sorry? Why or why not? Is it easy to forgive someone who has done something to you? Why or why not? Is it better to say you are sorry or to show you are sorry in some way? Should people be forgiven, if they do not say they are sorry and are not willing to change their ways? Which is easier, to forgive or to forget?

Is it a good idea to have a special time each year to say sorry and make up with friends/family? Is it a good idea each year for people to stop and think about what sort of person they are/how they might change to become a better person/whether they are making a success of their lives? What does it mean to be successful? Is it important to be successful? Why or why not?

The people of Nineveh were said to be evil. What does it mean to be evil? Is the world today an evil place? What makes you think this? Why do people do evil actions? Should everyone be forgiven regardless of what they have done? Are there some actions that are so evil they are unforgivable?

Title	**Exploring Christian beliefs about creation**
Broad stage	P7–S2
Targets	Be able to discuss issues such as the creation ... at a simple level but in response to their own questions and opinions (*Christianity*, Level E). Recognise and discuss interpretations of creation stories – literal and symbolic (*Personal Search*, Level E). Discuss the importance of beliefs about the origins of the universe ... as a basis for religious and moral thinking (*Personal Search*, Level F).
Key terms and concepts	God, creation, origins, awe and wonder, truth, praise and stewardship.
Background Information	The first line of the Apostle's Creed states 'I believe in God, Father almighty, maker of heaven and earth.' This belief in God as creator of the universe is a fundamental part of Christianity. The main source of these beliefs is Genesis 1 where we find a number of beliefs about God, the universe and human beings. God – There is a single God who created all life and who is in total control of his creation. God is isolated and unique, entirely distinct from the natural world that is completely subordinate to him. God is to be thought of as powerful but also benevolent. The universe – The world did not come about by chance, it was created on purpose. The world that God has created is orderly and has pattern and meaning. It is also organised hierarchically with God at the top and human beings as his deputies on earth. The world is said to be 'very good.' Human beings – They are the climax of creation and are created on the sixth day. They have been granted dominion over all other animals. The world is to be treated with respect. Human beings do not own the world; they are mere stewards. Christian beliefs about creation raise the important issue of the origins of the universe. Was it in fact created by an all-powerful being or did it come about by chance? Is there evidence of a 'designer' who planned the world? One of the most popular arguments for the existence of god has always been the argument from design. When we look around the world we find so much that is beautiful and ordered that we feel bound to say that it must have been created or designed. In nature the various parts of the body of humans and other living creatures are so well suited to fulfil their respective functions, it seems only logical to conclude that 'Someone' must have designed them for those purposes. The argument from design takes the order and apparent purpose in the world, and moves from that order and purpose to suggest a designer, God, who is responsible for it. The most famous form of the design argument was set out by William Paley in the eighteenth century (see Appendix 5 pp. 75–76). Through this topic pupils should also begin to appreciate how belief that God is Creator has an impact on the way Christians respond to the created world. Christians believe they should give praise to God and as stewards of the created world should care for and look after it for future generations. Pupils might also consider how for some Christians the idea of an ordered world is a basis for belief in God. The personal search aspects of the exemplar focuses on discussing questions and issues relating to the themes of origins, truth and care of the environment.
Assessment	This should relate to the personal search target on beliefs about the origins of the universe. At the end of the unit pupils could be asked to give a considered written response to the issue of whether the universe was 'designed' or came about by chance.

Finding out

Pupils could look at extracts from Psalms and/or hymns (see Appendix 5 p. 76) and listen to music written in response to the created world such as Haydn's creation and identify the feelings and beliefs of the writers about the created world. They could discuss the meaning of the word 'praise'. They could write their own psalm/hymn/music of praise.

Introduce the idea of a creed as a declaration of beliefs. Discuss with pupils the meaning of the opening statement of the Apostle's Creed. Help pupils become familiar with the Genesis 1 Creation story through pupils producing a mime/dance or a group book (a page for each day) or writing a version for younger readers. With support, pupils could examine the text of the story and in a series of bullet points identify key beliefs or be given a number of belief statements and match a statement to a verse in the text. They should consider the different ways in which Christians interpret the genesis story literal and symbolic.

Pupils could discuss a version of the argument for the existence of God from design (see Appendix 1e) and identify examples of pattern and order in the world. They should also consider examples of disorder, for example they could watch a video of a news extract about a natural disaster and discuss how this might counter the argument from design.

Discuss with pupils what Christianity teaches about human responsibility for the created world. Pupils could identify issues of concern regarding the environment today and in groups research an issue in depth and make a presentation. A class debate on 'humans are good stewards and managers of the world' could be held.

Making connections

Pupils could identify times they have been praised. Why? How did it make them feel? They might think of moments in their own lives when they have experienced something like awe or wonder, and share these moments. They could describe the moment in a piece of personal writing, explaining the impact it made on them and why it was unforgettable.

Working in groups they could prepare a presentation on the theme 'What we find amazing about the world'. In pairs, they could identify questions about things that puzzle them regarding the world. Pupils could respond in groups to one of the questions with a mind/concept map.

In the context of thinking about responsibility for the environment, they could devise their own action plan for treating the world with respect by writing 10 statements beginning with 'I will ... I won't'.

Thinking it over

Did the world have a beginning? How did the world come into being? Does the world have a purpose? Does the universe reflect a designer or random chance? What makes you think this? Does it matter? Is there a God?

Virtually all religions and cultures have an account about the beginning of the world? Why do you think this is? Is the account in Genesis 1 true? Are scientific accounts of the beginning of the world true? What does it mean to say something is true?

Are humans more important than the rest of creation? What responsibility do humans have for plants and animals? Are humans doing a good job at looking after the world? Why or why not? Do we have a responsibility for looking after the world? In what ways can we show respect and care for the world? What do we do that harms the world? What more could we do to care for the world? Can individuals really make a difference?

Title	**Muhammad, the Prophet of Islam**
Broad stage	P7–S2
Targets	Show some understanding of the special significance of key figures in the beliefs of faith communities, e.g. Muhammad as Prophet of Islam (*Other World Religions*, Level D).

Understand terms such as ' prophet' (*Other World Religions*, Level E).

Recognise that for many people religious beliefs provide a sense of meaning and purpose in life (*Personal Search*, Level E). |
| **Key terms and concepts** | Qur'an, Hadith, prophet, authority, guidance, call, vocation, role model/exemplar, meaning and purpose. |
| **Background information** | When Muhammad was a young man he went to work in the city of Mecca for a rich widow called Khadijah. His job was to look after the camels and caravans. Even at that time Mecca was a very important city. In particular it was home to the Ka'ba, the sacred house said to have been built by Abraham. It was filled with pagan idols worshipped by Arabian tribes who visited Mecca regularly on pilgrimage. When he was 25 years old Muhammad married Khadijah. As a result he became a wealthy and respected member of Meccan society. However he was uncomfortable with the pagan worship that went on in Mecca and spent more and more of his time in the hills and mountains meditating. On one occasion about the age of 40, while meditating in a cave outside Mecca, he encountered an angel sent by Allah. The angel ordered Muhammad to read but Muhammad said he was unable to read. However the angel insisted and Muhammad received his first message directly from Allah. He was to receive many more over a period of years. Muslims believe these messages make up what is now known as the Qur'an.

In his last sermon, shortly before he died the Prophet Muhammad said to his followers ' I leave behind me two things, the Qur'an and the example of my life. If you follow these you will not fail ….' For Muslims the Qur'an is the Word of God as revealed to the prophet Muhammad. It is their guide. It gives guidance on every important aspects of life and covers areas such as ethics, social justice, political principles, law, morality, trade and commerce. Islam means submission, and Muslims submit to the will of God. The will of God is revealed to them in the Qur'an. The Qur'an has authority over the lives of Muslims who try to be obedient to its teaching and, because they believe it contains the Word of God, they treat it with great respect. They also handle it with care and reverence.

The Hadith is a collection of Traditions about the Prophet Muhammad. It records his words and actions. For Muslims Muhammad demonstrated in practice what the Qur'an tells about in theory. The Hadith shows Muhammad as a person of compassion, kindness and wisdom. After the Qur'an, the Hadith for Muslims is the second fundamental source of guidance.

The personal search aspect of the exemplar focuses on discussing questions and issues relating to the themes of guidance and role models/exemplars. |
| **Assessment** | Pupils could identify beliefs and values that they think would have an important influence on a Muslim's sense of meaning and purpose and explain why. |

Finding out

Muhammad the Messenger
Tell pupils the story of the call of Muhammad to be a prophet. Pupils could sequence the story from a number of given episodes. Pupils could read about Muhammad's message in Makkah and summarise it in a series of bullet points.

Use the story of Bilal (see Appendix 5 pp. 76–77) to help pupils appreciate the different responses to Muhammad in Makkah. Pupils could produce a wanted poster showing the reasons for the opposition to Muhammad in Makkah, and why he had to leave.

The Message: The Qur'an
Pupils could play chinese whispers to help understand the idea of oral transmission and after investigation design a flow chart to show the story of the writing down of the message.

Introduce pupils to Sura 1 (see Appendix 5 pp. 76–77) and identify what it teaches about Muslim belief, especially the phrase 'guide us in the straight path'. Pupils could use a searchable database of the Qur'an (see Appendix 5 pp. 76–77) and find key teachings in the Qur'an, or be given quotes on beliefs, practices, family and social life and match a quote to a theme.

Muhammad the exemplar: The Hadith
Discuss with pupils why Muhammad as a businessman was given the names 'the trustworthy one'. Pupils could devise an acrostic on the word 'trust'.

Pupils could look at sayings of Muhammad (see Appendix 5 pp. 76–77) and choose one they think is relevant for today's world. Pupils could read an extract about the character of Muhammad (see Appendix 5 pp. 76–77), list the words that describe his character and choose the five qualities they think are the most important. They could find out why the letters 'pbuh' are used in Muslim books about Muhammad.

Making connections

Muhammad the messenger
Discuss with pupils times they have been 'chosen' to do something. Introduce pupils to someone who believes he/ she has been chosen by God and discuss the implications of this belief.

Using newspapers as a stimulus, pupils could discuss what a modern day prophet might challenge in society today.

The message: The Qur'an
Explore what a guide does, thinking of a tour guide, a mountain guide. Pupils could write a description of 'the ideal guidance teacher', contribute to a class display of guide books and discuss whether a book can be an effective guide.

They could contribute to a class guide book to help a new pupil settle in. Discuss with pupils what guides them when making important decisions and what topics an effective guide for life might contain.

Introduce the idea of authority by identifying people and institutions with authority and discuss whom or what has to be obeyed in today's world.

Muhammad the exemplar: The Hadith
Pupils could brainstorm a list of role models/heroes and produce a class display. In groups produce a list of qualities/ attributes of a good role model. They could identify for each member of the class a name that describes a positive aspect of their character – such as 'Joan the caring one', 'Matthew the generous one'.

Thinking it over

Is it important that people have a guide for life? Why or why not? What guides and influences you? How do we decide what is the right thing to do? Where might we go to find advice on what to do? How do we decide what advice is worth following? Should anyone or anything tell us what to do and how to live our lives? Why or why not?

Is it important that we have 'role models' to look up to and examples to follow? Why or why not? Whose example do you follow? What is it about them that you admire? How much should we allow others to influence us? Are you a role model for anyone? Are you a good role model? What makes you think this? What might others learn from the way you live your life?

Religious and Moral Education: Personal Search

Part 4: Appendices

Appendix 1: HMI on Personal Search

In one primary school HMI concluded in their report that 'within the personal search aspect of the programme, pupils had not developed the skills of reflecting on religious ideas.'

In another they recommended that 'teachers should adopt a wider range of methods to give pupils more opportunities to research information and discuss their views on religious beliefs, practices and issues.'

Commenting on some of the best practice HMI stated with regard to one primary school that 'at all stages almost all pupils showed very good awareness of important moral issues and relationships and were able to express themselves well in aspects of Personal Search.'

As one of a series of reports dealing with individual subjects in the secondary school HMI have recently published 'Standards and Quality in Secondary Schools: Religious and Moral Education 1995–2000. The report is based on inspections of 76 departments in secondary schools over a period of five years. The report states: 'Many S1/S2 courses did not make effective provision for 'personal search', the element that encourages pupils to reflect upon, discuss and analyse ideas and concepts. Courses generally consisted of a series of units that provided little progression and coherence. Teachers took too little account of pupils' prior experience leading to a lack of continuity between primary and secondary. In the best practice, courses provided well-structured investigations of a breadth of religious belief and practice, together with opportunities for pupils to reflect upon religious interpretations of the meaning and purpose of life. The best courses also encouraged pupils to discuss and analyse important moral issues.'

There was a need for:
- more opportunities for pupils to reflect upon questions about meaning, value and purpose in life
- the development of analytical and evaluative skills
- reducing the dependence on worksheets and using more varied resources including visits and visitors
- better account to be taken of pupils' experiences and achievements in the primary school.

Appendix 2: Stories from world religions

A.   Muhammad and the Cave P1–P3

At first the religion of Islam was no more than a small number of people led by a man called Muhammad. They lived in Mecca, a city in present day Saudi Arabia. Muhammad believed that there was only one God, Allah. This belief brought him and his followers into conflict with the rich merchants who ruled Mecca. They believed in many gods and they made huge profits from the fact that thousands of people came every year to worship the statues and idols of the gods that were kept in a sacred building known as the Ka'aba. The rich merchants had no desire to see Muhammad becoming popular. They were afraid that if people began to believe there was only one god they would stop coming to Mecca and the merchants would lose all their profits. So they decided to get rid of him once and for all.

One night they sent some men to kill him. But Muhammad had been told of the plan and he had already escaped along with his friend Abu Bakr. They journeyed far into the mountains where they knew they could find a good hiding place and be safe from those who wanted to kill them. Meanwhile a reward of one hundred camels was offered to anyone who could capture Muhammad and bring him back. A hundred camels was worth a lot of money in those days. Eventually Muhammad and his friend found a cave that seemed to them to be an ideal place to hide. It was dry and gave them shelter from the cold night air. Within a few days friends arrived with a supply of food. Despite this, however, Muhammad and Abu Bakr were still very frightened. If their friends could find them so could their enemies.

It was then that an amazing thing happened. A spider started to spin its web across the mouth of the cave and doves built a nest on the floor near the entrance. Shortly after this, Muhammad and Abu Bakr heard the voices of those who had been trying to kill them. They were looking among the rocks and searching the nearby caves. When they saw the spider's web across Muhammad's cave they thought that there could not possibly be anyone in there. They were even more convinced when they saw a dove flying out of its nest at the entrance to the cave. As a result they did not bother to search it. Muhammad and Abu Bakr were saved.

B.   The Story of Joseph P4–P6

The story of Joseph is part of the long history of Judaism that begins with Abraham. Abraham had became dissatisfied with the many gods associated with his homeland in Mesopotamia and he left home to search for what he believed was the one true God. Abraham's grandson, Jacob, had twelve sons whose families later became the twelve tribes of Israel. One of Jacob's sons was called Joseph.

When the story begins Joseph is about seventeen years old. Jacob was a very old man by the time Joseph was born and because of this Jacob seemed to love Joseph more than any of his other sons. He had even given Joseph a special present, a beautiful long robe with sleeves, something he hadn't given to any of his other sons. As you might imagine none of this went down well with Joseph's brothers. In fact they were extremely jealous of him. They hated the sight of him and they hardly ever spoke to him.

To make matters worse, Joseph announced one day to his brothers that he had had a dream. In his dream he was working in the fields with his brothers binding up the sheaves of corn. All of a sudden the sheaves that Joseph was binding stood upright. His brothers' sheaves then gathered round them and bowed down as if they were in the presence of a king. Joseph certainly had a very high opinion of his own importance. 'Who does he think he is?' said his brothers, and they hated him even more because of this.

One day Jacob suggested to Joseph that he should go and join his brothers who had taken their flocks far away from home in order to find good pasture land. Joseph agreed and set off for a place called Shechem where his father said his brothers would most likely have gone. When his brothers saw him coming in the distance they began to talk amongst themselves about the possibility of getting rid of him. 'Why don't we just kill him and throw him into a pit', said some of the brothers. 'We could say that a wild animal had got him.' 'No', said the other brothers, 'we can't kill him, after all he is our brother. Why don't we just throw him into the pit and leave him there.' And that 's exactly what they did. When Joseph arrived they immediately took off his fine robe with the long sleeves that his father had given him and threw him into a pit.

But just then they spotted a caravan of traders with their camels carrying goods to Egypt. One of the brothers said, 'I know, let's sell him to the traders.' The other brothers quickly agreed. So they took Joseph out of the pit and sold him to the traders for 20 shekels of silver. Then they took Joseph's robe and covered it with the blood of a goat. They took the robe home to Jacob as proof that Joseph had been killed.

C.   The Story of Kisa Gotami P7–S2

Buddhists do not worship a person or a god but follow a system of beliefs, meditation and spiritual exercises based on the teachings of the Buddha. The Buddha taught that all our thoughts and actions have consequences both for ourselves and for others. This law of cause and effect, known as karma, says that the consequence of good deeds, words and thoughts is rebirth into a better life. In the same way, when those who do not accept personal responsibility for the things they do in life are reborn, they will find they are further away from that state of happiness and peace Buddhists call Nirvana.

In the Buddhist scriptures there are many stories about the Buddha's attitude to death and rebirth. The story of Kisa Gotami tells how the Buddha helped a woman come to terms with the sudden death of her son. At first she was full of grief and refused to accept that her son was dead. She went from door to door visiting all her neighbours and begged them to give her something., some medicine that would restore her child to health. Her neighbours did everything they could to comfort her but there was nothing they could do to bring her dead son back to life. Kisa Gotami was unconsolable.

Just as she was about to give up one of her neighbours suggested that she go and talk to the Buddha who was at that time teaching in the area. Exhausted, she set off and eventually found the Buddha. 'Do you have any medicine that would help my son,' she pleaded. The Buddha looked with compassion on Kisa Gotami and the dead son she was carrying in her arms. 'I do know of something that will help you,' he said, 'mustard seeds. Go to the village and ask for mustard seeds. But you must only take mustard seeds from households in which no one has died.'

Kisa Gotami did as she was told and returned to the village. She was certain she would be able to get the precious mustard seeds. Knocking at the first door, she asked for the mustard seeds. ' Certainly' said the young woman who answered the door, 'I've got plenty'. As Kisa Gotami was about to take the seeds she remembered the instructions that the Buddha had given her. 'Before I take the seeds' she said, 'I must ask a question. Has anyone died in this house?' The young woman looked surprised. 'Why, yes, my husband's mother died only a few months ago'. Kisogotami knew she couldn't take the seeds and moved on. At the next house an old man answered the door. He also had plenty of seeds, but recently his wife had died. At the next house, a young man answered the door and was willing to give Kisogotami some seeds, but his father had just died. Kisa Gotami went further into the village. At every house the answer was the same. They had seeds, but she could not find a house where no one had died.

With a heavy heart she returned to the Buddha and said 'Sir, it is impossible to get the mustard seeds you told me about. In every home there are plenty mustard seeds. But I could not find one house in the whole village that had not at some time had a member of their family die. The Buddha replied, 'You had imagined that in the whole world only your son had died. You thought that only you had been touched by death. Now you know that death is with us all'.

Kisogotami finally agreed to have the funeral arrangements made for her child. She had finally accepted the death of her child. Later she returned to listen to the Buddha teaching and eventually became a follower.

Birth of the Buddha

A long time ago in northern India there lived a king and queen. The king's name was Suddhodana and the queen was called Maya. One day the Queen had a strange dream. She dreamed that a beautiful white elephant danced before her holding a lotus flower in its trunk. The elephant then seemed to enter the right side of her body. She went to the king and told him all about her dream. He immediately called together his priests and advisors. They interpreted the dream as meaning that the king and queen were to soon to have a son who would be very special. He would either be a king who would rule over all the world or a holy man who would become a great religious leader.

When it was nearly time for the baby to be born the Queen and her husband went to visit her parents. But before they could reach the place where her parents lived the baby was born. The king and queen called their son Siddhartha. He was born in the middle of a beautiful grove of trees in a place called Lumbini. A wise man called Asita, one of the king's special advisors, came to see the baby. He said that the baby would, without doubt, grow up to be a very great man. Siddhartha had beautiful long fingers and toes and a smooth, golden coloured skin. He had a very unusual sign of a wheel on his foot and soon after his birth had taken seven steps very firmly and steadily.

When the king and queen returned to their kingdom everyone was happy and there were great celebrations all over the land. But the king was worried. He remembered what all his priests and advisors had told him about his son becoming either a great ruler or a holy man. He loved his son very much and did not want to see him grow up just to leave home and become a wandering holy man. He wanted what he thought was best for his son. He wanted him to become a great king. So he decided to keep him in the palace for as long as he could in order to prevent him from seeing what the world was really like. He gave him all sorts of toys and games to play with so that Siddhartha would not want to go outside the palace. He also gave him the best of clothes and the best food to eat.

Guru Nanak and the twenty rupees

A long time ago in an area of India still known today as the Punjab there lived a boy called Guru Nanak. He lived with his father, mother and sister in a comfortable house in the country. He was a very special boy and everyone liked him. He was always ready to help other people, especially the children who worked in the fields. They were poor and often hungry and Nanak would invite them to his house to eat.

When he was about 15 years old his father said to him, 'Nanak, you will soon be a man and you will have to get a job like everyone else. I want you to get some experience of the kind of things you will have to do. The first job I want you to do is to go into the fields and look after the cattle.'

So Nanak did what he was told and went off into the fields but he was not really interested in looking after cattle. He preferred to spend his time talking to the Sadhus or holy men and sitting under his favourite tree meditating and praying to God. When his father found out what Nanak was doing he became very worried. Not only would Nanak soon be grown up but he would eventually get married. How could he look after a wife and children if he had no job and was unable to earn a living?

So Guru Nanak's father decided that he must teach Nanak how to make money. He gave him 20 rupees and told him to go to the town and buy things, then sell them on at a profit. Nanak set off for the town. As he got near to the town he met a group of sadhus sitting in the shade under a large tree. They looked very thin and weak and their clothes were in tatters. 'You look hungry and tired', said Guru Nanak, 'when did you eat last?' 'Four days ago', said the one of the sadhus. 'We only eat when God provides us with food.'

Immediately Guru Nanak knew what he had to do. He went straight to the town market and spent the whole of the twenty rupees on food for the sadhus. He bought so much food that he had to hire a cart to carry it back to where the sadhus were sitting. When the sadhus saw all the food they were amazed. 'Thank you', they said, 'you are so kind. May you be happy for the rest of your life.' When Nanak arrived home and told his father what he had done his father was furious. 'I give you money and you spend it on a few old sadhus. How can you waste your money like that feeding the hungry. You will never have good clothes and a fine house if you carry on like this. When will you ever learn' 'Father,' said Guru Nanak, I understand what you want me to do. But God wants me to do things in a different way. He wants me to help others whenever I can.

Krishna and his two sisters

A long time ago in India there lived a boy called Krishna. He was no ordinary boy because he had been sent into the world by the God Vishnu. Krishna had two sisters. One was his real sister, Subhadra. The other was his adopted sister, Draupadi.

The two sisters were not at all alike. Subhadra never seemed to be happy. She was always complaining and grumbling about something. And she was jealous of her sister because she believed that Krishna loved her more and spent much more time with her. Draupadi, on the other hand, was kind and generous and never talked about her sister behind her back.

One day Subhadra said to Krishna, 'You should love me more than Draupadi because she is only your adopted sister. I am your real sister.' Krishna replied, 'If I seem to love Draupadi more than you, perhaps that is because she seems to love me more than you do.' This made Subhadra very angry and she refused to speak to Krishna.

Not long after this Krishna had an accident. He cut his hand quite badly and it would not stop bleeding. He ran into the house and found Subhadra. 'Will you help me,' Subhadra, my hand is bleeding.' Subhadra glanced quickly at his hand but said there was nothing she could do. Leaving Krishna alone she went off to find a bandage.

Some time passed and Subhadra had still not returned. When Draupadi arrived and saw Krishna's hand she immediately tore a piece off her sari and wrapped it tightly around Krishna's hand to stop the bleeding. And she spoke gently to him to reassure and comfort him. Eventually the bleeding stopped.

Subhadra, however, never did come back either with the bandage she had promised or even to find out if he was all right.

A day in the life of a Buddhist monk

4.00 – 4.30 a.m: I get up.

5.00 – 6.30 a.m: I go to the community's first meeting at five o'clock. We start this by lighting candles and bowing to the shrine three times. For about 30 minutes we chant, thinking about the qualities of the Buddha – his kindness, wisdom and compassion. Then we sit in silent meditation for about an hour. At the end of the meditation the senior monk rings a bell, and we bow to the shrine three times to end the meeting.

6.30 – 7.15 a.m: After the meeting I go to the room in the community where I work preparing leaflets for all the people who visit us in the day. I might also do a little tidying up.

7.15 – 8.30 a.m: At 7.15 a.m. I go to the main hall for some tea. All the monks are there and the abbot usually announces what jobs have to be done that day and then he usually gives a talk about Buddhist teachings.

8.30 – 10.30 a.m: I am free to choose what to do I usually do my laundry or go for a walk or have a chat with someone or write a letter.

10.30 a.m – 12.00: A bell is rung at 10.30. It is time for our one meal of the day that has to be eaten before noon. I put on my robe, take my alms bowl and go to the hall. The food has been given to us by lay people. I put what I need in my bowl and go and sit on the floor. We then chant that is a traditional way of saying thank you to the people who gave us the food. After the meal I wash my bowl and go back to my room.

12.00 – 1.30 p.m: I've been up quite a long time so I usually have a rest.

1.30 – 7.15 p.m: This is my work time so I go the office to work. I am quite good on the computer and might spend time preparing a leaflet about our day. I usually try to get out for a walk. I enjoy being out in the open air. Later in the afternoon I meet up with other monks for a cup of tea and a chat.

7.15 – 9.00 p.m: At seven fifteen the bell is rung and I'll go to the hall for the last meeting of the day. We chant for about half an hour and them meditate for about an hour. Sometimes the abbot will give another talk about Buddhist teachings.

9.00 – 10.00 p.m: Back to my room to read or write a letter.

10.00 p.m: Bed and sleep.

The story of the two brothers

This story is about two brothers living on a farm who shared the work and the harvest. One of the brothers who was unmarried was concerned about his brother who was married and had two children, wondering if they had enough to eat. He secretly one night decided to help his brother and put into his brother's store six bags of corn to help him. The married brother on the same night was thinking what a lucky person he was – a wife, children and corn in the barn. He thought of his brother all on his own and decided that as an acknowledgement of his good fortune he would make his brother a gift of six bags of corn and secretly put them in his brother's store. Next day, each brother went to their store and were surprised to see each still had the same number of bags as before, but they didn't say anything to each other. They kept quiet about what they had done. From then on at harvest time each brother secretly moved six bags of corn into the other brother's store. Of course, the next morning they both found exactly the same number of bags of corn as they had started with. Neither brother ever found out why this happened.

A fuller version of the story can be found in the book *Stories from the Muslim World* published by MacDonald.

Muslim Aid

Address: PO Box 3, London, N7 8LP
Web: www.muslimaid.org.uk

A saying of Muhammad

'Every person's joint must perform a charity everyday; to act justly between two people is a charity; to help a man with his mount, lifting him on to it is a charity; a good word is a charity; removing a harmful thing from the road is a charity.'

Appendix 5: Sources for P7–S2

Blowing in the Wind – a Jewish story

As an introduction to the main themes of Yom Kippur pupils might explore a children's story told at Yom Kippur 'Blowing in the Wind'. Versions of it can be found on websites about Yom Kippur.

The story is about a man who went to the Rabbi at Yom Kippur to apologise, because he had been gossiping about the Rabbi and spreading false rumours. The man said he would do anything if only the Rabbi would forgive him. The Rabbi said he should take a feather pillow into the city, wait for the wind to blow and then let all the feathers out. He should then collect them and bring them back to the Rabbi. The task of course was impossible. The man said 'But they'll go everywhere – there's no chance I'll be able to gather them up'. 'Exactly', said the Rabbi, 'it's the same with gossip and spreading rumours – they go everywhere and they are hard to clean up.'

The ritual of the scapegoat (Leviticus 16:20–22)

A goat will be chosen and Aaron, the Priest, will place both his hands on the goat's head and he will confess all the evils and sins of the people of Israel. The sins and evils of the people will be transferred to the goat. The goat will then be driven off into the desert and the sins and evils of the people will be carried away into an uninhabited land.

An argument from design

Suppose you are walking across a heath, says William Paley, and you knock your foot against a stone. You might think, if you were to think about it at all, that the stone had always been there. This would, in the circumstances, be a very logical answer. But if you were to come across a watch, then you would naturally ask where the watch had come from. You would not in this case naturally conclude that it had always been there. You would wonder who had made the watch and for what purpose. You see that it is working, the hands are moving. You open the back and see the intricate mechanism that makes the watch work – cogs and springs. The pieces of the mechanism were carefully planned and put together to make the watch work. You conclude that the watch has been designed. It did not come about by chance.

Paley uses this story as an analogy for the universe. Like the watch, the universe requires a creator or designer to explain its existence, because it is just as complex a mechanism, even more so. For Paley then, the universe resembles a watch in its organisation and complexity, although on a much greater scale. Its existence can only be explained by reference to some external intelligence. Surely, therefore, there must be a cosmic designer who has made and arranged the world the way it is for a purpose.

Others often quote the eye as an example. It performs an important function. It is a wonderful organ. It can recognise colour. It can focus on objects near and far away. It is wonderfully made. Just as there is no chance the watch came about by chance, so it is impossible the eye came about by chance. The eye is even more complicated than a watch. The eye therefore must have been designed and made by a craftsman. This designer and maker of the eye and of the entire world is what people call 'God'.

Psalms and hymns of praise

Psalm 8
Psalm 19:1–4
Psalm 95
Psalm 104 (selected verses)

Possible hymns/songs that might be used are
My God I thank thee who hast made (verse 1)
For the beauty of the earth
Praise to the Lord, the Almighty, the King of Creation/Morning has broken.

Muhammad

A Qur'an database can be found at islamcity.com/mosque/quran/ Pupils might be encouraged to find teaching about beliefs such as God, Creation, Paradise; practices such as fasting, prayer, charity and pilgrimage; and beliefs about family and social life such as marriage, food, intoxicants, ambling, divorce and parents.

Extract from Sura 1
'In the Name of God, the Merciful, the Compassionate
Praise belongs to God, the Lord of all Being,
The All-merciful, the All-compassionate
The master of the Day of Judgement
Thee only we serve
Guide us in the straight path'.

Some sayings of Muhammad from the Hadith
'None of you is a true believer until he wishes for his brother what he wishes for himself.'
'Part of someone's being a good Muslim is his leaving alone that which does not concern him.'
'He is not a believer who eats his fill while his neighbour is hungry.'
'Whosoever of you sees an evil action, let him change it with his hand, and if he is not able to do so, then with his tongue, and if he is not able to do so, then with his heart – and that is the weakest of faith.'
'He who has no compassion for our little ones, and does not acknowledge the honour due to our elders, is not one of us.'
'No one has eaten better food than what he earns with the toil of his own hands.'
'The earth is green and beautiful and Allah has appointed you his steward over it.'

The Character of Muhammad
'During his lifetime, Muhammad (PBUH) demonstrated a noble and exemplary character. He was an absolute believer in one God, and was thoroughly trustworthy in respect of his companionship, help and guidance. He was affectionate, kind and sympathetic to his compatriots: always considerate, truthful and sincere, perfectly faithful in respect of all trusts and promises. He kept himself aloof from gambling, drinking, vulgar wrangling and all the vices

that were rampant among the people of his time. He was fair and honest in his dealings; generous and obliging to his friends and benefactors. The Prophet's life, therefore, became the model and perfect example for all Muslims and for all times to come. To follow his Traditions along with the guidance of the Qur'an is every true Muslims's earnest ambition.' (Extract from RE Briefs on Islam: A Guide for Teachers prepared by the Religious Education Support Service of the Islamic Foundation)

The story of how Muhammad was called to be a prophet can be found in 'A Tapestry of Tales' from Palmer, Sandra, and Breuilly, Elizabeth, *Religion for Education and Life: Story Resource Pack* published by Collins Educational, 1992, ISBN 0 00 3120007

The story of Bilal can be found in the magazine *RE Today* spring 1996 edition. This story tells how Bilal, a slave, was persecuted by his master for becoming a follower of Muhammad.

Religious and Moral Education: Personal Search